Spells

WESLEYAN POETRY

Spells

NEW & SELECTED POEMS

ANNIE FINCH

WESLEYAN UNIVERSITY PRESS

Middletown, Connecticut

Wesleyan University Press
Middletown CT 06459
www.wesleyan.edu/wespress
© 2013 Annie Finch
All rights reserved
Manufactured in the United States of America
Typeset in Galliard by Tseng Information Systems, Inc.

Wesleyan University Press is a member of the
Green Press Initiative. The paper used in this book
meets their minimum requirement for recycled paper.

This project is supported in part by a grant from the
National Endowment for the Arts.

Library of Congress Cataloging-in-Publication Data
Finch, Annie, 1956–
[Poems. Selections]
Spells: new and selected poems /
Annie Finch. — First edition.
pages cm. — (Wesleyan Poetry Series)
ISBN 978-0-8195-7269-1 (cloth: alk. paper) —
ISBN 978-0-8195-7363-6 (ebook)
I. Title.
PS3556.I448S64 2013
811′.54—dc23

2012044385

5 4 3 2 1

CONTENTS

As long as I can remember, my life has been dedicated to poetry—to dreaming, hearing, reading, and making poems. *Spells* gathers the most important of this poetic work written over four decades, from 1970 to 2010. In addition to selections from my books *The Encyclopedia of Scotland* (1982), *Eve* (1997), *Calendars* (2003), and *Among the Goddesses: An Epic Libretto in Seven Dreams* (2010), *Spells* collects many new and previously unpublished poems, including "The Lost Poems," experimental, metrical poems from the 1980s that did not find their audience until the recent embrace of formal poetic strategies by avant-garde poets.

The poetry in *Spells* is organized into sections by decade. Rather than grouping the poems according to the books in which they first appeared, I have chosen to arrange the poetry so that readers can follow its unfolding in reverse chronological order. The two short final sections, of translations and performance work, are arranged in chronological order and will spiral you forward again. The collection includes lyric and narrative poems, performance texts, verse drama, translations, libretti, chants, rituals, elegies, sonnets, villanelles, ars poetica, epithalamia, valentines, prayers, letters, dialogues, pastiche, and other shapes. Most of the poems are spoken in ancient and contemporary rhythms: sapphics, cretics, dactyls, amphibrachs, trochees, anapests, folk stanzas, iambs, and others.

The book's title, *Spells*, captures my sense of poetry as a performative art—patterned language that invites readers to experience words not just in the mind but in the body. The title also points to the spiritual foundation of my aesthetic. As a Wiccan, I write poems as incantations to strengthen our connections to each other, to the passage of time, and to the sacred cycles of nature.

Compiling this book has led me to appreciate how much I was inspired as a poet by coming of age during the feminist movement of the 1970s. Reading it has helped me understand the ways I struggled over the years to throw off the burden of misogyny on my spiritual, psychological, intellectual, political, and poetic identities. My themes are often female-centered: sexuality; friendship; childbirth, breastfeeding, mothering, and abortion; sexism and incest; women's mythology and spirituality; and personal and cultural foremothers. I am proud to define myself as a woman poet. Women's poetry, from the ancient Sumerian Enheduenna to Dickinson and her neglected "poetess'" sisters and daughters, including Osgood, Dunbar-Nelson, Teasdale, and Millay, and forward through Bishop, Plath, Bogan, Helen Adam, H.D., Brooks, Kizer, and Lorde, has been critically important to me (along with, of course, the work of many beloved male poets). In my current lyric, narrative, and epic poetry, as well as in my dramas and libretti, my ambition is to create a body of work for a re-emerging matriarchal culture.

Throughout my career, I have collaborated with other artists, on architectural and visual installations, musical settings and opera, drama and performance poetry, and translations. My aim as a translator is to embody the spirit of the original poems within their original formal constraints (e.g., Akhmatova's amphibrachs, Labé's rhyme schemes, Sappho's sapphics), allowing the reader to experience the poetry's original shapes. In my dramatic pieces, I am drawn to mythopoetic theater's blending of spoken language with music, choreography and masks, to enact a ritual journey toward psychological and spiritual power.

Compiling *Spells* has been a transformative experience that has filled me with gratitude to the fierce and accepting Muse who has whispered poetry into my meditative darkness over the past half-century. I invite the reader to speak these poems aloud (even if only in the mind), and to be open to the spells they cast.

Portland, Maine
June 2012

New Poems

These are the hours to revel in.

.

BLESSING ON THE POETS

Patient earth-digger, impatient fire-maker,
Hungry word-taker and roving sound-lover,
Sharer and saver, muser and acher,
You who are open to hide or uncover,
Time-keeper and -hater, wake-sleeper, sleep-waker;
May language's language, the silence that lies
Under each word, move you over and over,
Turning you, wondering, back to surprise.

HOMEBIRTH

Home is a birthplace since you came to me,
pouring yourself down through me like a soul,
calling the cosmos imperiously
into me so it could reach to unroll
out from the womb where the wild rushes start
in a quick, steady heartbeat not from my own heart.
This is my body, which you made to break,
which gave you to make you, till you bear its mark,
which held you till you found your body to take,
(open at home on my bed in the dark).

ABORTION SPELL

Let's keep the world through its own balanced kiss,
the kiss come from women made of our own blood,
the holder, the cooler (redeeming the earth,
shaping the room where we give you your birth).
Hands born of woman will not stop this flood,
this generous, selfish, long-opening gift.

As I went walking in the land of our heart,
I found the animals crying.
Their mouths and warm bodies were sudden and slow
And they moved slow and hard to the edge of the woods.
Their legs and their heartbeats and skins were dying.
They curled up like snails at the end of the world.

This land is your land, this land is my land.

As I went out walking, the trees became bark.
They turned in their power and knowledge and pain.
Their arms grew wide open, their lives fell apart.
I heard them in peace and I heard them in horror,
And each leaf or hand was the eye of a world.

This land is your land, this land is my land.

As I went walking by the side of the sea,
I found the waves understanding.
They rolled out of silence and into the mist,
And into the light where it seemed they were pouring.
They roiled with pollution and anger and love,
And the currents of freedom kept rolling.

This land is your land, this land is my land.

STONE AND CLOTH AND PAPER

> *At every gust the dead leaves fall*
> —*Henry Wadsworth Longfellow, "The Rainy Day"*

Two close centuries of stone and cloth and paper
chalked your cheeks and carved your hands to broken.
You are not a monument any more, now—
more like a forest

moving shadows under simple trees, dark rivulets
mottling snow fading in this warm gray winter,
melting the centuries you didn't know, Henry Longfellow—
wait—I can hear you—

a low and earnest voice, wind in fir trees, burning
through this room, where you wrote your saddest poem,
through this house, where the farm and family built you.
Your sister Ann's portrait

stumbles, eyes black as night behind a candle.
The marble urn in your red brick yard has fallen,
knocked down in the emptiness of the fountain.
Cries of the seagulls

reach through walls to find you again, pour down
the carrying knowledge that grew your branching gardens—
and tell me which old words, which new wings, will carry
you from this courtyard.

THE NAMING

Lopez, Jurgens, Lozowsky, O'Connor, Lomax
(Shoes, and spirals, dust, and the falling flowers)
Díaz, Dingle, Galletti, DiPasquale,
Katsimatides

Wounds widen the remembering earth.
Closed eyes see beyond the flames.
Grief opens hands to feel the wind.
Heart beats like ocean and hears the names:

DiStefano, Eisenberg, Chung, Green, Dolan,
(Women running suddenly in their high heels)
Penny, York, Duarte, Elferis, Sliwak,
Yamamadala,

Closed eyes see beyond the flames.
Grief opens hands to feel the wind.
Heart beats like ocean and hears the names.
Wounds widen the remembering earth:

Weinstein, Villanueva, West, Sadaque,
(Spirals, dust and spiraling dust and hours)
Bowman, Burns, Kawauchi, Buchanan, Reilly,
Reese, Ognibene,

Grief opens hands to feel the wind.
Heart beats like ocean and hears the names.
Wounds widen the remembering earth.
Closed eyes see beyond the flames.

Kushitani, Ueltzhoffer, Wong, Ferrugio,
(Breathed in only in or beyond the naming),
Inghilterra, Tzemis, Liangthanasam,
Coladonato—

Heart beats like ocean and hears the names.
Wounds widen the remembering earth.
Closed eyes see beyond the flames.
Grief opens hands to feel the wind.

Sanchez, Talbot, Afflito, Siskopoulos
(Every question with a long sob of naming)
Tarantino, Zempoaltecatl, Thorpe, Koo,
Stergiopoulos,
Zion, Zinzi, Song, Shahid, Santiago,
Ortiz, Pabon, Ou, O'Neill, Newton-Carter,
Miller, Mohammed,
Zakhary, Campbell,
Deming, DiFranco,
Chowdhury, Blackwell,
Zucker, McDowell,
Goldstein, Basmajian . . .

Wounds widen the remembering earth.
Closed eyes see beyond the flames.
Grief opens hands to feel the wind.
Heart beats like ocean and hears the names.

FROST'S GRAVE

I think of your quiet grave now and again
When innocence has rolled me out of sleep
Close to my husband's side, to lean again
Against his breathing human side, to keep
Myself breathed in his liquid human breath.
I think of your nurturing grave so often. Death
Has made you a place I like to imagine going:
Opening the gate to your grave, entering in,
Reaping your silence where a small tree, growing
Generous in the forgiveness of your sin,
Leans over your stone, the grass, your bones, the grass,
The grass. The grass. I like to imagine frost there, hung
Like frost on a beach in November, when the sun
Rises on winter, just as it rose on spring,
On the humid decision to grow, past everything.

TAROT: THE MAGICIAN CARD

Rain wets the wand, wind moves a sword,
lightning lights crystal where the thundering cup
forms me a channel and takes on a word,
pouring the pentacle I gather up.
Time carves the storm in the palm of my hand,
till it fills with shapes that send me down
through my river-body. Do I stand
at a table the waiting planet surrounds?
Through my own fingers, eyes, and palm,
and through other worlds, huge or small,
one fury spins and turns me calm;
I breathe and watch it land and fall,
holding what I hardly know or see,
filled with the storm that makes, makes me.

KEYS

Phi Beta Kappa poem, Yale University, 2011

Like an island, a key makes a door. In the surge
Of its mineral clarity, seas come unbound.
Though an arch curves together, the keystone will stay
Braced in gravity, locked by immensity, wound
To a temple in air by the spiraling play
That could tumble much heavier forces. What's found
Past the musical notes that cascade and converge
In a key, past the tock the tick carries away
When it's wound by a key? There are patterns that merge

Meanings, silent until we code them open,
Clued to us by the random knowing tribes:
Carvings, letters, hands, faces, symbols, stars.
Each warm friction's vibration circumscribes
One more seat in the clearing where we are
Gathered, circling a home we can't describe.
What's the word but a word that can't be spoken?
Who'd tear pleasure out past life's iron bars?
Where's the use of a code that won't be broken?

A ring of keys hangs like a question at your side.
You move through the answering darkness like a key,
While windows of moonlight branch down the catacombs
And rustle each prisoner into mystery.
Each lock, like each room, is alone till the opening comes;
Your ring reaches one, then another. Liberty
Repeats down the corridor, doors pulled open wide,
Exploding more showers of sweetness through the combs
Whose locks had been waiting for one key to be tried.

BEACH OF EDGES

A drift of snow edges a new drift of sand
As edges grow deeper. It's March, month of edges.
Wet rocks yield to pebbles like opening hands.

The glisten of rockweed trails, splutters, and bends,
And sparkles of rivulets bounce down in ledges.
A drift of snow edges a new drift of sand;

It's March, month of edges, and I'm left to stand
Alone outside time as new light pulls and nudges
Wet rocks. Yield to pebbles like opening hands,

Light; pull me from winter. How have I planned
For light that's not winter, for live light that fledges
A drift of snow, edges a new drift of sand

Beyond my last sight, and waves me like a wand
Out back over the surges of these rocking sedges?
Wet rocks yield to pebbles like opening hands;

I want to go back to him, as to the land;
light, carry me over from the wild old grudges.
A drift of snow edges a new drift of sand;
Wet rocks yield to pebbles like opening hands.

EARTH DAY

All we want is to find the love
in the faces of the people we love.
All we need is to find the dark
in the nighttime sky, to lie down to sleep
in the darkness, where stars and moon keep vigil,
in the silence of a sleeping earth.
All we require is to wake to sunlight
in the morning, to simple sky,
to breathe aloud as the sky is breathing,
to drink the water of the earth.

All we need is to touch the planet
and find it clean where we were born,
where our ancestors breathed and planted,
where we live with the plants and birds.

All we need is to live with the memory
of a future we want to imagine.
All we want is to find the love
in the face of the planet we love.

REVELRY

Chairs root. Their trunks are runged with snow.
Curtains grow velvet thick, like bark,
in this warm landscape ringed with dark.
Is passion only revelry?

Voices believe words and move free.
Lust moves our lips. Blood fills our skin.
We bend alive around cup and cloud.
These are the hours to revel in.

ARCHITECTURE

Proportion is life measured open by harmony.
It vaults us to open like atriums, entering
our pillared awareness in footsteps, then building
our spaces with conscious decision. Its mystery
makes earth that our forest looks back for. Its beauty
has felt us repeating, then come to repeat us.
Its answers have carved us like mineral and bent us
in spirals. Its questions have rocked us past symmetry.
And, if we have voices that build to a word
and breathe out through poems, it comes to enclose us
by seeding the places we know we inhabit—
(make local, remember, name, touch and are stirred
in, share with those who understand, love, or oppose us
(because they live here, in the place we inhabit,
and believe what we have grown wise believing:
that belief, like love, rests on no foundation
but the shapes we know how to make by knowing
how they enclose us))—
how they unfold us.

Poems, 2000–1990

Point your fire like a flower.

WATCHING THE WHALE

A hard gray wave, her fin, walks out on the water
that thickens to open and then parts open, around her.

Measured by her delved water, I follow her fill
into and out of green light in the depth she has spun

through the twenty-six fathoms of her silent orison,
then sink with her till she rises, lulled with the krill.

Beads of salt spray stop me, like metal crying.
Her cupped face breathes its spouts, like a jewel-wet prong.

In a cormorant's barnacle path, I trail her, spun
down through my life in the making of her difference,

fixing my mouth, with the offerings of silence,
on her dark whale-road where all green partings run,

where ocean's hidden bodies twist fathoms around her,
making her green-fed hunger grow fertile as water.

PARAVALEDELLENTINE: A PARADELLE

For Glen

Come to me with your warning sounds of the tender seas.
Come to me with your warning sounds of the tender seas.
Move me the way the seas' warm sea will spend me.
Move me the way the seas' warm sea will; spend me.
Move your sea-warm come to me; will with me; spend
tender sounds, warning me the way of the seas, the seas.

Tongues sharp as two wind-whipped trees will question.
Tongues sharp as two wind-whipped trees will question.
(Skin or nerve waiting and heart will answer.
Skin or nerve waiting and heart will answer).
Question will answer two tongues and, or will:
heart sharp as nerve trees; waiting, skin-whipped wind.

Brim your simple hand over where the skin is.
Brim your simple hand over where the skin is.
Wish again, whenever hair and breath come closer.
Wish again, whenever hair and breath come closer.
Closer, again, whenever; brim where your skin is;
hair, wish and breath over the simple hand, come.

Spend come warning me, whenever simple sounds will, will;
move your question. Answer your heart-sharp tender
sea-warm will with me. Way of the seas, the seas!
Where skin-whipped nerve trees wind over waiting tongues,
brim closer to me. Again the skin, as wish,
and two of the breath, hand and hair, or come, is.

WILD YEASTS

For Marta

Rumbling a way up my dough's heavy throat to its head,
seeping the trailed, airborne daughters down into the core,
bubbles go rioting through my long-kneaded new bread;
softly, now, breath of the wildest yeast starts to roar.
My hands work that peaked foam, push insides out into the light,
edge shining new sinews back under the generous arch
that time's final sigh will conclude. (Dry time will stretch tight
whistling stops of quick heat through my long-darkened starch.)

How could I send quiet through this resonant, strange, vaulting roof
murmuring, sounding with spores and the long-simple air,
and the bright free road moving? I sing as I terrace a loaf
out of the hands it has filled like a long-answered prayer.
Now the worshipping savage cathedral our mouths make will lace
death and its food, in the moment that refracts this place.

EARTH GODDESS AND SKY GOD

You haven't formed me. I'm a monster still.

Then give me your body. Give it to me in rain.

Look up and fill me. I am too dark to stain.

You haven't held me. I hold apart my will

Spread dryness through me. I have a night to fill

in high heat-speckled waves, apart from where

I will come down. I have nothing to share

with breath. I will give it back. There is one to kill,

one to renew, and one to persuade to weep.

My night holds everything except for sleep.

CONVERSATION

Edward Weston's "Squash," 1936

"Delve for me, delve down, delve past your body, crowned
by its hidden stem, like a shadowy alarm;
see how you vanish past our dark-shed charm,
throat over throat, ankle to ankle, bound
in our different arches, summer-nicked and browned
interlocking rings in the chain of wrist and arm."

"Lie for me, lie. I want to feel you turn.
Mark out the summer's bending month and learn
to cradle the concrete ground till it softens. Stay.
Measure me past my stem. Though your shadows churn,
close yourself over. Encompass me like clay."

CALENDARS
A poem in chants for four voices:

Demeter

        Chorus
        Persephone

                Hades

In the winding
of the vine
our voices stretch
from us and twine —

No, going into the waiting places
is not easy. Flowers fade there.

around the year's
fermented wine —

Mostly, it's surrender of wanting,
or the fear that a flame will be dampened—
or that everything warm will come rushing
over me with reproach—or that endless

needles could be ranged in the tunnel—
or that my bare feet would be slippery—

Yellow. Fall roars
down to the ground,
loud, in the leafy sun that pours
liquid through doors.
Yellow, the leaves go down

or that once I'm down in that darkness
someone outside will block off the entrance—

Touches of gold stipple the branches,
promising weeks of time —

Thread with Me

My lover, when you riddle with me—

reddening slowly, then suddenly free,
turned like a key

Oh! the falling flowers have caught me
by dipping yellow, purple towards the hunger—

—the hard, the intricate dark
(I hear the notes of your words
ring for me cool as the birds,

my lover—

through the long year's
fermenting wine

her thin stems turning, held to be—lost—

my lover, when you thread with me

Now you are uncurled and cover our eyes
with the edge of winter sky,
leaning over us in icy stars

through this night-shot

night-shot dark

is never easy.

Flowers fade here.

Voices pull me on through the cavern
from the new season. Her voice old, silent—

our hands, our breasts, our curves
curl through our hands and ravel—

On damp limestone, a violet curling—

my lover, when you riddle with me
the hard, the intricate dark.

Rack me with courage, spring,
come kill me, flowers;

if we are shadows, come;

make me our shadows

as I reach for flowers.

OVER DARK ARCHES

Naked and thin and wet, as if with rain,
bursting I come out of somewhere, bursting again.
And like a great building that breathes under sunlight
over dark arches, your body is there,

And my milk moves under your tongue —

where currents from earth linger under cool stone
rising to me and my mouth makes a circle
over your silence

You reach through your mouth to find me —

Bursting out of your body that held me for years,
as the rain wets the earth with its bodies —

And my thoughts are milk to feed you

till we turn and are empty,

till we turn and are full.

A CAROL FOR CAROLYN

> *It is easy to be a poet,*
> *brim with transparent water.*
> —Carolyn Kizer, "In the First Stanza"

I dreamed of a poet who gave me a whale
that shadowed clear pools through the kelp-making shade.
When beached sea-foam dried on the rocks, it would sail
down currents that gathered to pool and cascade
with turbulent order.
She brims with transparent water,
as mother and poet and daughter.

The surface is broken and arching and full,
impelled by the passions of nation and woman.
The waves build and fall; the deep currents pull
toward rocky pools cupping the salt of the human.
The ocean she's authored
brims, with transparent water,
for poet and mother and daughter.

CHAIN OF WOMEN

These are the seasons Persephone promised
as she turned on her heel;
the ones that darken, till green no longer
bandages what I feel—

Now touches of gold stipple the branches,
promising weeks of time
to fade through, finding the footprints
she left as she turned to climb.

GHAZAL FOR A POETESS

Many the nights that have passed,
But I remember
The river of pearls at Fez
And Seomar whom I loved.
— "Laurence" Hope, 1903

The corners of the frontispiece yellow from their darker edges.
Aching eyes lift in tremolo from their darker edges.

Moon lit your blood in the jasmine-blooming gardens;
bodies still glide in tableau from their darker edges.

Your "hungry soul" laps at the page with its "burning, burning";
your moans send out an echo from their darker edges.

Silk covers your arms, your fingers, your lips, your voice.
Your black lines weave a trousseau from their darker edges.

Wind strikes at the palm trees where you walked;
fronds shake like tousled arrows from their darker edges.

Your nights spread quiet over "parched and dreary" sand.
Finches fill them till they glow from their darker edges.

MEETING MAMMOTH CAVE,
EIGHT MONTHS PREGNANT

In the night to my humanness
the unparticled has poured,
no beam will sink or angle,
no slow new mineral drip
through the circling ceiling

(loud strength of a darkness
only dark can reassure

(solid cavern's holding,
to hollow the beautiful

carrying dark to hold me,
to empty the slippery

(The loud strength of a darkness
only dark can reassure

(solid cavern's holding,

No beam will sink or angle,

open cavern's holding,

in the rock to my humanness
unparticled and poured

to hollow the beautiful

(Into no circumference.

BUTTERFLY LULLABY

My wild indigo dusky wing
my mottled, broad-wing skipper,
a sleepy, dreamy dusty wing,
flying through my night.

My northern, southern, cloudy wing,
my spring azure, my crescent pearl,
a silver-spotted, sweet question mark,
sleeping in my sky.

A tiger swallowtail, harvester,
moving through my hours,
an eyed brown in the redwing dark,
wrapped softly in my words.

INTIMATIONS OF PREGNANCY

I never thought that this immediate

A groping fist would prove me what I am

I am not a woman

My vigil is too restless

I never thought till now I could be had.
I can't forget you, that's the awful thing.

I am not a woman.
I curse what I have been

I am solidifying like a rock
That turns inside itself each time she turns

WALK WITH ME

Walk with me just a while, body of sunlight,
　body of grass, surface of trees,
head bending to the earth we have tasted,
　body of death, surface of leaves.
Sinking hooves in the mud by the river,
　root of the live earth, live through my body.
Sinking body, walk in me now.

TWO BODIES

Two bodies, balanced in mass and power,
move in a bed through the dark,
under the earliest human hour.
A night rocks, like an ark.

They reach through the ceilings of the night,
tall as animals.
Through their valleys bends the light
of their fertile hills.

Two bodies breathe their close hellos
through interlocking pores,
while that hush of beating slows,
held, with many oars,

heart over heart, leg over leg,
trading still breath, until,
heart over heart, and seed into egg,
night holds two bodies still.

FINAL AUTUMN

Maple leaves turn black in the courtyard.
Light drives lower and one bluejay crams
our cold memories out past the sun,

each time your traces come past the shadows
and visit under my looking-glass fingers
that lift and block out the sun.

Come—I'll trace you one final autumn,
and you can trace your last homecoming
into the snow or the sun.

ELEGY FOR MY FATHER

HLF, August 8, 1918 — August 22, 1997

Bequeath us to no earthly shore until
Is answered in the vortex of our grave
The seal's wide spindrift gaze towards paradise.
—Hart Crane, "Voyages"

If a lion could talk, we couldn't understand it
—Ludwig Wittgenstein

Under the ocean that stretches out wordlessly
past the long edge of the last human shore,
there are deep windows the waves haven't opened,
where night is reflected through decades of glass.
There is the nursery, there is the nanny,
there are my father's unreachable eyes
turned towards the window. Is the child uneasy?
His is the death that is circling the stars.

In the deep room where candles burn soundlessly
and peace pours at last through the cells of our bodies,
three of us are watching, one of us is staring
with the wide gaze of a wild, wave-fed seal.
Incense and sage speak in smoke loud as waves,
and crickets sing sand towards the edge of the hourglass.
We wait outside time, while night collects courage
around us. The vigil is wordless. And you

watch the longest, move the farthest, besieged by your breath,
pulling into your body. You stare towards your death,
head arched on the pillow, your left fingers curled.
Your mouth sucking gently, unmoved by these hours
and their vigil of salt spray, you show us how far
you are going, and how long the long minutes are,
while spiraling night watches over the room
and takes you, until you watch us in turn.

Lions speak their own language. You are still breathing.
Here is release. Here is your pillow,
cool like a handkerchief pressed in a pocket.
Here is your white tousled long growing hair.
Here is a kiss on your temple to hold you
safe through your solitude's long steady war;
here, you can go. We will stay with you,
keeping the silence we all came here for.

Night, take his left hand, turning the pages.
Spin with the windows and doors that he mended.
Spin with his answers, patient, impatient.
Spin with his dry independence, his arms
warmed by the needs of his family, his hands
flying under the wide, carved gold ring, and the pages
flying so his thought could fly. His breath slows,
lending its edges out to the night.

Here is his open mouth. Silence is here
like one more new question that he will not answer.
A leaf is his temple. The dark is the prayer.
He has given his body; his hand lies above
the sheets in a symbol of wholeness, a curve
of thumb and forefinger, ringed with wide gold,
and the moment that empties his breath is a flame
faced with a sudden cathedral's new stone.

SAMHAIN

October 31

In the season leaves should love,
since it gives them leave to move
through the wind, towards the ground
they were watching while they hung,
legend says there is a seam
stitching darkness like a name.

Now when dying grasses veil
earth from the sky in one last pale
wave, as autumn dies to bring
winter back, and then the spring,
we who die ourselves can peel
back another kind of veil

that hangs among us like thick smoke.
Tonight at last I feel it shake.
I feel the nights stretching away
thousands long behind the days,
till they reach the darkness where
all of me is ancestor.

I turn my hand and feel a touch
move with me, and when I brush
my young mind across another,
I have met my mother's mother.
Sure as footsteps in my waiting
self, I find her, and she brings

arms that have answers for me,
intimate, a waiting bounty.
"Carry me." She leaves this trail
through a shudder of the veil,
and leaves, like amber where she stays,
a gift for her perpetual gaze.

WINTER SOLSTICE CHANT

December 21

Vines, leaves, roots of darkness, growing,
now you are uncurled and cover our eyes
with the edge of winter sky
leaning over us in icy stars.
Vines, leaves, roots of darkness, growing,
come with your seasons, your fullness, your end.

IMBOLC DANCE

From the east she has gathered like wishes.
She has woven a night into dawn.
We are quickening ivy. We grow
where her warmth melts out over the ice.

Now spiral south bends into flame
to push the morning over doors.
The light swings wide, green with the pulse
of seasons, and we let her in

We are quickening ivy. We grow

The light swings wide, green with the pulse

till the west is rocked by darkness
pulled from where the fire rises.
Shortened time's reflecting water
rakes her through the thickened cold.

Hands cover north smooth with emptiness,
stinging the mill of night's hours.
Wait with me. See, she comes circling
over the listening snow to us.

Shortened time's reflecting water

Wait with me. See, she comes circling

A SEED FOR SPRING EQUINOX

March 21

. . . till I feel the earth around the place my head has lain
under winter's touch, and it crumbles. Slanted weight of clouds.
Reaching with my head and shoulders past the open crust

dried by spring wind. Sun. Tucking through the ground
that has planted cold inside me, made its waiting be my food.
Now I watch the watching dark my light's long-grown dark makes known.

A WREATH FOR BELTANE

May 1
[Three voices, alternating stanzas, repeating poem at least three times]

May is here, come around,
Find a place on the ground.

Find a place on the ground,
and the flowers rain down.

And the flowers rain down.
We are gorgeous today.

We are gorgeous today,
We're alive for the May.

We're alive for the May,
May is here. Come around.

SUMMER SOLSTICE CHANT

June 21

The sun, rich and open,
stretches and pours on the bloom of our work.

In the center of the new flowers,
a darker wing of flower

points you like a fire.

Point your fire like a flower.

LAMMAS

August 1
[two voices, alternating]

Fill the earth's belly full.

> Fill the earth's belly full.
> Bring the food, bring the grain.
> There are cold months ahead.
> Give them peace in the ground.

Bring the food, bring the grain.

> Fill the earth's belly full.
> Bring the food, bring the grain.
> There are cold months ahead.
> Give them peace in the ground.

There are cold months ahead.
Give them peace in the ground.

> Fill the earth's belly full;
> bring the food, bring the grain.
> There are cold months ahead.
> Give them peace in the ground.

A MABON CROWN

September 21

Our voices press
from us
and twine
around the year's
fermenting wine

Yellow fall roars
Over the ground.
Loud, in the leafy sun that pours
Liquid through doors,
Yellow, the leaves twist down

as the winding
of the vine
pulls our curling
voices —

Glowing in wind and change,
The orange leaf tells
How one more season will alter and range,
Working the strange
Colors of clamor and bells

In the winding
of the vine
our voices press out
from us
to twine

When autumn gathers, the tree
That the leaves sang

Reddens dark slowly, then, suddenly free,
Turns like a key,
Opening air where they hang

and the winding
of the vine
makes our voices
turn and wind
with the year's
fermented wine

One of the hanging leaves,
Deeply maroon,
Tightens its final hold, receives,
Finally weaves
Through, and is covered soon

in the winding
of the vine—

Holding past summer's hold,
Open and strong,
One of the leaves in the crown is gold,
Set in the cold
Where the old seasons belong.

Green and red are here,
orange and gold,
yellow, maroon, and bronze, all near,
lost by the year,
lost, all that fall can hold.

Here is our crown
Of winding vine,
Of leaves that dropped,

That fingers twined,
Another crown
To yield and shine
With a year's
Fermented wine.

LETTER FOR EMILY DICKINSON

When I cut words you never may have said
into fresh patterns, pierced in place with pins,
ready to hold them down with my own thread,
they change and twist sometimes, their color spins
loose, and your spider generosity
lends them from language that will never be
free of you after all. My sampler reads,
"called back." It says, "she scribbled out these screeds."
It calls, "she left this trace, and now we start"—
in stitched directions that follow the leads
I take from you, as you take me apart.

You wrote some of your lines while baking bread,
propping a sheet of paper by the bins
of salt and flour, so if your kneading led
to words, you'd tether them as if in thin
black loops on paper. When they sang to be free,
you captured those quick birds relentlessly
and kept a slow, sure mercy in your deeds,
leaving them room to peck and hunt their seeds
in the white cages your vast iron art
had made by moving books, and lives, and creeds.
I take from you as you take me apart.

Water that moves, in a bodylike stream,
through its cool channels fills the warm prairie's dream.
Waking to tend it, the grass-moving sky

pours with grasses. Big Bluestem's drinking roots lie
nine feet down the waving, remembering sod
they have swum through, to feed on, to build. When it swings
like a wing in small flight, when it sways,
turkey feet murmur, red three-toed feet sing.

Little Bluestem, as copper as autumn or clay,
floating seeds past the prairie's dense, watery hand
till they shimmer to columns, wet smoke on the land;

Indian Grass, lapping up the spattering sun;
prairies step slower than palaces, down
under the teeming roof of the ground,
quiet as animals. Then, when they rise,
prairies, like palaces, loom, and surprise.

IOWA BARN

Light and shadow
frame a window
that comes reaching
past a roof-edge
and becomes a hole. Sky goes
funneling to
any darkness,
cut by warped
wooden framing,
long-abandoned
by the glass that
could reflect us.

BLUET

Inevitable, the body of the world
weeps in inventive dust for the hiatus
that winks above it, bluet in your breasts.
 —*Hart Crane, "For the Marriage of Faustus and Helen"*

Since the hiatus between all the searching
opens wherever I want it to go,
and since I am made of a body that ages
already wept for, and already gave
up for you, listen, and just once please fall
down to my hands; let this weeping be all:

Lost with your body in fog once, we counted
beating cascades all the way up to clouds,
then looked up slowly and found that before us
hung one blue flower. We spoke it aloud:
"Bluet." We spoke it, knowing it would last

as long as the blue in the reckoning sky
arching down to us. Then we saw the petals
pull from their center and not one would stay
(Yes, I am listening, answered the bluet;
that's what I wanted, and now I will fall.)

Hoping for you now, we cry in our bright
glittered hexagonals, swept by the sound
of lost-ashore music with rain falling down,
our tears building dust into patterns that carve
trails to the solace, the stars of your breasts
(Dust is always the language we use.)

LANDING UNDER WATER, I SEE ROOTS

All the things we hide in water
hoping we won't see them go—
(forests growing under water
press against the ones we know)—

and they might have gone on growing
and they might now breathe above
everything I speak of sowing
(everything I try to love).

CHANGING WOMAN

If we change as she is changing,
if she changes as we change

(If she changes, I am changing)

Who is changing, as I bend
down to what the sky has sent us?

(Is she changing, or the same?)

SPIDER WOMAN

Your thoughts in a web have covered the sky.
A thread from the northwest is carrying beads from the rain,
a thread from the southwest is carrying beads from the rain,
a thread from the southeast carries bright beads,
a thread from the northeast is bringing the beads
of the rain that has filled up the sky.
Spider, you have woven a chain
stretching with rain over the sky.

APHRODITE

Aphrodite, come to me,
even while I lie resting with my infant.
Cover me with your sweet certainty.

EVE

When mother Eve took the first apple down
from the tree that grew where nature's heart had been
and came tumbling, circling, rosy, into sin,
which goddesses were lost, and which were found?
What spirals moved in pity and unwound
across our mother's body with the spin
of planets lost for us and all her kin?
What serpents curved their mouths into a frown,
but left their bodies twined in us like threads
that lead us back to her? Her presence warms,
and if I follow closely through the maze,
it is to where her remembered reaching spreads
in branching gifts, it is to her reaching arms
that I reach, as if for something near to praise.

INANNA

A young goddess, full of love, fresh with the touch of a husband,
carrying power and rich with anger, strength, urgency, understanding,
follows the direction her ear has led her, down to the place where the
    underworld glistens.

At each door she removes a jewel, a belt, a ceremonial robe.
At each door, she is less and more. She bows down through the
    seventh door.

The young goddess is dead, and waiting. The young goddess is dead.
A goddess goes down, and I can see her. She needs to go, decides
    to go.
A goddess goes down, and I can hear her.

COATLIQUE

She listens for breathing
around her in the night.
Below the mountain,
families are sleeping.
When will she wake
to bring the morning?
When will she birth
sun and stars?
When will her mist
give birth to the moon?

The skulls are breathing,
as quiet in her necklace
as darkness will keep them.

NUT

I cry for my lost days, I cry for my childhood,
I cry for the goddess coming down from the sky.
I cry for a place on the ground for my feet
and I call for a place on the ground for my hands.
In the daylight my hands reach out for home;
in the night, the stars connect the stones
and find their way. The shooting stars
fall from your breasts, your arms.

BRIGID

Ring, ring, ring, ring! Hammers fall.
Your gold will all be beaten
over sudden flaming fire
moving from you, the pyre. Sweeten
your cauldron, until the sun
runs with one flame through the day
and the healing water will sing,
linger on tongues, burn away.

RHIANNON

A child is ranging, like a young horse;
a child is growing, like a gray mare.
She carries the coastal wind in her teeth
and the furious sun in her mane.

RUNNING IN CHURCH

For Marie

Then, you were a hot-thinking, thin-lidded tinderbox.
Losing your balance meant nothing at all. You would
pour through the aisles in the highest cathedrals,
careening deftly as patriarchs brooded.

You made the long corridors ring, tintinnabular
echoes exploring the pounded cold floor,
forcing the walls to the truth of your progress:
there was a person in this church's core.

Past thick stained-glass colors wafted and swirling
in pooled interludes that swung down from the rafters,
cinnabar wounds threw light on your face, where the
pliant young bones were dissolving in laughter.

BLOOD CHARM:
FROM THE MENSTRUAL HUT

How can I listen to the moon?
Your blood will listen, like a charm.

I knew a way to feel the sun
as if a statue felt warm eyes.
Even with ruins on the moon,
your blood will listen, every time.

Now I am the one with eyes.
Your blood can listen, every time.

ENCOUNTER

Then, in the bus where strange eyes are believed to burn
down into separate depths, ours mingled, lured
out of the crowd like wings—and as fast, as blurred.
We brushed past the others and rose. We had flight to learn,
single as wings, till we saw we could merge with a turn,
arching our gazing together. We formed one bird,
focussed, attentive. Flying in silence, we heard
the air past our feathers, the wind through our feet, and the churn
of wheels in the dark. Now we have settled. We move
calmly, two balanced creatures. Opened child,
woman or man, companion with whom I've flown
through this remembering, lost, incarnate love,
turning away, we will land, growing more wild
with solitude, more alone, than we could have known.

GULF WAR AND CHILD: A CURSE

He is sleeping, his fingers curled,
his belly pooled open, his legs gathered, still
in their bent blossom victory.

I couldn't speak of "war" (though we all do),
if I were still the woman who gave birth
to this soft-footed one: his empty hand,
his calling heart, that border of new clues.

May the hard birth our two heartbeats unfurled
for two nights that lasted as long as this war
make all sands rage, until the mouth of war
drops its cup, that bleeding gift we poured.

BEING A CONSTELLATION

Heavy with my milk, you move
your compact body, though I hold
you dense under a constellation
whose sparse lights ache over you.

If, looking up, you recognize
the shadowing of curves that cast
down towards my belly, and the way
my nipples travel, like two stars

twinned by your eyesight; if my arms
take night, and keep it from the sky,
if my night voice can stop your cry,
I'll be the Mother over you.

You are a question, small and dense,
and I am an answer, long diffuse
and dark— but I want to be sky
for you so, like the stars, I lie,

holding my far lights wide and flat
in pictures for your eyes to take,
spaced easily, so you can catch
the patterns in your sleepy net.

MY RAPTOR

My mind hovered over my baby, like
a raptor, and froze everything it saw.
I looked through my own pregnant belly's raw
perimeters and found his heart to strike
attentive until, helpless with the pound
of still more blood, he seemed to settle down.
It was my loss to feel like god alone
for a new one always listening, to reach
inside for his ears to share the flying speech
I heard so constantly. Within my grown
silence, my sounding, my loud body where
the baby turned, my mind learned not to care
whether thoughts I felt he noticed with no fear
were mine alone — or whether he could hear.

THE WISH FOR EYES

On solid hills through liquid dusk,
the city turns to rise

with its purple touch, to enter me.
I touch it with my eyes.

Righted with wrongs, or even hard,
Let me be made of eyes.

Gray nature, make a dusk of me,
and let me keep my ties.

THE LAST MERMOTHER

I used to fish in San Francisco Bay,
without a net, for love as well as food.
Out by the water, on a long, cool day,
I had a place to go, and some time to brood.
The only woman usually, I glued
my hands to the rod. Men left me alone; I enjoyed
those days, until the day I was destroyed.

It started with a tentative tug, slow, confined
without a glance or the pressure of a hand.
Then it teased me like a simple, other mind
across my own, vibrating with command.
Then I almost fell, as she charged high and fanned
open her tailfins, arching through the spray
of her own raging white wake. Don't look away!

Listen. I breathed, and she tore away the line
and raised her face—her empty eyes—beside
the dock. She howled, stretching her hand to mine,
floating her tail in the rocking of the tide
as she clung to the slippery post below. I tried
to look at her. I saw that it was true.
Well, what would you have done? I helped her through

the railing. Draped with clammy seaweed strands,
she wiggled her huge shoulders through and lay
flopping along the pier, with those open hands
still held towards me. Now I know that was the day
I lost my mind. She's followed me the way
a beggar could haunt a doorway. She's in my shade
whenever I feel empty or afraid.

Look at her now; by now she's growing old.
We hear her every night, that singing, through
the heartless air, carried on the cold
enchantment of the California dew,
futile and endless notes, a wordless clue
poured out over the deafened land. I wish,
sometimes, I'd thrown her back in like a fish,

when I saw her breasts. A mother! I still can't say
if my fishing hook killed it, or if she
dropped it in the struggle, but of course it died that day.
And I know wherever it fell, there must be
a shrinking in the waves, the hissing sea,
a crust of sand still thickening on the edge
of its quiet bones.

TRIBUTE

You'll find it — when you try to die —
— Emily Dickinson

When there are no words left to live,
I have elected hers

to haunt me till the margins give
and I am left alone.

One voice has vanished through my own
To make me like a stone,

one that the falling leaves will sink
not over, but upon.

THE INTELLECT OF WOMAN

> *The intellect of man is forced to choose*
> *perfection of the life or of the work.*
> —Yeats, "The Choice"

The intellect of woman must not choose
perfection of the life, or of the work.
Perfection has a diamond for a muse
who scratches where she only needs to look.

And yet the intellect of woman fears
imperfection's lonely grandeur, with the sharp
delight of knowledge that pushes through her ears,
the edge that cuts her vision from the dark.

an enlightenment of excising

So the intellect of woman will not mind
some scratches where the diamond's edge has moved.
Perfection's habit opens us to find
cuts in a window we have never loved.

NOT PERFECT, BUT FORGIVEN.

73

MOON

Then are you the dense everywhere that moves,
the dark matter they haven't yet walked through?

No, I'm not. I'm just the shining sun,
sometimes covered up by the darkness.

But in your beauty—yes, I know you see—
There is no covering, no constant light.

Poems, 1989–1980

The peace under water
is not like sleep.

COURTSHIP

Courtship is pulling with your full-moon heart
to bring out patterns. Patterns dry, crisp tides
that crescent up the beach, past sifted sand,
as sunset comes. When all the shores are dark,

night pulls with courtship's tides (Love leaves the tides
aside, to push on further up the sand,
to change far pools, to ebb into the heart
of earth and leave it salty, full, and dark)

Walking changes as dusk starts to gather.
We're not able or sure anymore.
We don't know the path—and if we did know it,

we wouldn't go on. We're afraid of the dark
lowering its heavy, long familiarity
down on the grass. We're afraid of the night,

moonless, desert, California,
making us stumble. We shouldn't be lost,
out here like demons just at the border

that touches us solid, as if we were gone.
She's leading me on a path as narrow
as sisters can share. We pound back down the mesa.

Each of our feet finds its own way, delving
into the gulley whose trees never answer
until, with steps slapping soft as bandits,

I slow on the path, imagining horses.
Stretching necks right out of the stones,
out of the dusk where dark has achieved our
bodies, drawn by the strides that my sister

takes like a rider, Zaraf's Star,
Fashad, Kashmir, Arabian horses
raise her up with motionless shadow

so she can ride (like a rider, she walks),
cantering, encompassing the pace of the mountain.
Out in a landscape to curl or be curled in,

hunched like riders or curling like rides,
under the fairy-tale oaks of the mesa
that hide sleeping children or horses inside,

we talk about horses like hers who run carefully,
with thinner ankles, and mustangs who, fast,
wild grown, wild on the path to blackness,
hunger like stars reaching down for dark leaves.

GODDESS

The gravity of goddess is above
my eyes, when I look up like someone's child.
There is no spoken sentence. All she says
will die. It will be quiet when I go
out of the room and stop being a priestess.
She looks down. Her only death is unashamed,
undimming power like receding grain
that waves across my fields in shocking wav-
ing silence, beating in the window light.
She does not go to make new presences,
but stays to go. Her presence is the loss.
In the cold sky that waits each season out,
her body's ancient stars give restless calls
up to a throne that quivers in my heart
as fiercely in love as in the hate
on which thousands of years of sorrow fed.
Her birdsong joys shine ruins in my sky.
I seem to stand on some eternal plain,
watching the monuments that dawn again.
The gravity of goddess is above
my eyes, though never gone from history.
So many must have noticed, with this shock,
our patient looking up, and looking down.

PEARL

Reaching with eyes, they covered her as a girl,
leaving a grain of gaze, that irritant stare
women must cover everywhere, like pearl.

Even alone in her own room, she curled
back from the windows gleaming with their glare.
Reaching with eyes, they covered her, as a girl,

and stopped her eyes as their long look unfurled,
taking her in as if she belonged there,
a woman, covered everywhere, with pearls

draping her throat. And then she learned to whirl
before the mirror, pierce her ears, and twine her hair.
Reaching with eyes, they covered her, as a girl

covers herself and hunches to a coil
spiraling from the voyeur. But beware:
women cover everything, like pearls

orbed into life. A living ocean swirls;
we reach through it to spiral everywhere.
Reaching with eyes, they covered, in the girl,
what the woman covers: everything, like pearl.

INTERPENETRATE

Like the bleached fibers and their haunted ink,
interpenetrate each others' solitudes,

not penetrating, not dissolving; stay
rolled with the single patterns of the days,

linking through pages to burn with speaking lace
and thread to bodies, evenly alive.

STRANGERS

She turned to gold and fell in love.
She danced life upside down.

She opened her wild eyes again
and asked some strangers in.

The strangers felt her in and out.
They found her outsides thin.

Since her heart was still and hard,
they knocked her insides in.

INSECT

That hour-glass-backed,
orchard-legged,
heavy-headed will,

paper-folded,
wedge-contorted,
savage—dense to kill—

pulls back on backward-moving,
arching
high legs still,

lowered through a deep, knees-reaching,
feathered down
green will,

antenna-honest,
thread-descending,
carpeted as if with skill,

a focus-changing,
sober-reaching,

tracing, killing will.

THE GRIM GARDEN

Out of old earth that the worms ate
the grim garden began to grow
as peas, dull dragons, unwound and dipped
rough leaves the land had licked,

lulled with a lingering dust of crumbs
left by the tongue of the turned-up
underground dirt. Over the earth,
beans bent their bowed figureheads,

hunched so heavy, held so hard,
it filled them with force to face furrows,
send out the wings of their small sails
into the wind, and walk waves.

INSIDE THE VIOLET

Beside the long hedge on my parents' drive,
where the gravel waited daily for their tires
to crunch it open, in the narrow band
of earth along the hedge that kept the loam's
thick secret from the shifting sun, I knew
a purple violet. It always grew there,
hanging its knotty shoulders in the shade
of large, more splendid leaves, its crumpled head
releasing toward the earth.

One day I crouched
to find its eye much nearer than before
and stared inside. My own eye was lost
in the echoing hold of the raw deep I saw,
though my hands held back inside the driveway world
that slowed its pulse around me as loud sun
shattered all the gravel into shade
and tamped the earth. The middle of the violet loomed;
its heart was gazing into mine to hold
me like a violet, too. Then as its yellow, strong
throat turned to me and opened one more door,
defining light poured from a silent sun,
flooding my face and choking my eyes, until
I stopped looking in violets.

BLUE WILLOW

Once days blew in a pattern, when blue willows
bent where they blew, and bowls filled with birds
and plates arched out from them. Days blew across cups,
and covered the stories on saucers, and then the week came.

It's morning. Day rises above me,
and my own house, and the door, the tea in the cup
that you sip from, the blue willow china,
till more sun leans over the backs of the chairs —

SPEAK SOFTLY

The birds are everywhere, and hardly sing,
and I am anywhere, an only thing
(speak softly, and we do not own the land):

thin wind settled, spored on cotton sand
and convoluted. Wind over the land.
The birds are everywhere, and hardly sing.

I am a settler who was settled here
to speak and have no words about this land.
Its touch is built on shreds of spoken sand.

Its beat tells in sad bound and open hands.
Its old words sing in words my ears can't hear,
since they were spoken here, not anywhere,

and I am anywhere, an only thing,
while birds are everywhere, and hardly sing,
and my home fills me up with touching hands
I cannot touch—that never owned the land.

THE DOOR

It seemed as if a door came calling,
in a voice as old as carols,
telling lies as old as candles,
in words that were all about
some afternoons, lost on a child,
that could have been simple but
were lost, when I was just a child.

There was a day and then a dream
that I went through, and a cathedral
whose tall choir prayed
a singing message through the nave
until I heard a forest there
(though far outside, the trees were bare)

NO SNAKE

Inside my Eden I can find no snake.
There's not one I could look to and believe,
Obey, and then be ruined by and leave
because of, bearing children and an ache.

I circle down on Eden from above,
searching the fields in solitude and love
like a high hawk. He would never forsake

this place that's made again of memory;
he'd wait in that tree below me, spring
out towards my growing shadow, let it bring
a sudden hope that he could coil free—

but he's not there. Only the mountains that curve
and dip around the valley when I swerve
settle with dark heights, as I near the tree.

A SMALL SOUND IN THE DARK WOODS

She had run to just this point deep in the woods
when night overcame her eyes and even drowned
Apollo's footsteps, and she stopped and stood
just here while the wood closed into its circles
around her, and soon the shadows stopped moving.
Where I stand now to look around, she stood
and watched the circles stop above her head,
while far away in the loud rumbling leaves
whose patterned panic still reflected god,
his long pursuit, his blind abandonment,
his uncle's heavy tides, the celestial feet
that flew to bear his messages, and the wills
of the other gods, accompanying him like stone
that fell in sounds now in those pattering leaves,
it seemed she heard this sound, another breath,
moving in fingers where there is no wind
to make life out of leaves, or leaves from hands.
The ground is hard and covered with small stones
left from the river, where nymphs used to play
around those banks with Peneus, her father,
before he turned her to a laurel tree.
Now Peneus is gone, and the nymphs are still.
They won't come back. The ocean is far away.
Her roots are deep. Now nothing seems to move
in the continual evening of a night
where she can't sleep, and I can't close her eyes.
The woods are dark, and nothing in the sound
tells Daphne who it is that she hears breathe:
only these woods can hear her breath, my breath,
moving the leaves away from Daphne's hands.

From the Lost Poems

. . . you love in words, you don't know what you move

SUCH HUSKS

Such husks of hollowed influence. Such clear
thick patterns from the nights that held me full.
You keep your own still paces, with the last
touch of a spirit on you, like a down
that ripens, falling everywhere we pass.

NOW IN NOVEMBER

Now in November, as I face towards home
pulling my living behind me, and my dead,
the skulls of fire widen into a road.
November turns into a room of leaves
and lets them fall around him. Then he goes,
and where he stood, his body blank and bare,
only a halo of shocked twigs remains
spread on the still green, still elusive grass.

SONG OF THE SORRY SIDE

On the sorry, sorry side of the world
is an opening that hides the girl
who is closing up her heart.

She has fallen down a winding curve
to the place where solid seas are torn
and the continents are lost in stone
that obtrudes upon their rest.

When the lava reaches to the girl
burrowing around inside the world,
solid places in the ocean floor
fill the spaces she was looking for,

and the lava slowly rides the sea
till it reaches to her heart.

An opening has gone.
A rising has begun.

AWFUL FRIEND

To wake across the cold that holds the past
again. To see that once again, it lasts.
To waken with a nightmare and a smile
from someone who has been there a long while,
to watch again the lingering repast
he makes, that makes me his again at last,
to hurry, waiting only for the end
that he has picked you for—your awful friend,
in the dark maelstrom that he makes the past,
in the wide whirlwind that the present makes
as you keep waiting for his hand to break,
for the stiff rigid emptiness at stake
within my heart to make him fall and break.

NIGHTMARE

Opening light calls the river back to see
where the old nightmare has risen from, when she
calls herself back in the rhythm that is she.
Nightmare, oh woman lost in the depths of me,
lost to the rage that has risen up with me,
lost till I ride you home—nightmare of me.

RESOLUTION

I'll call those scattered parts back to my side,
and marshal them, so power cannot hide
so far inside its brow and cloudy skies;
I'll call the night attendants to put on
their green control and walk up to my side
with thin and arching tendons bending low,
speaking my parts, the ones they used to hide.

They will walk easily, for they have shown
the way to many easy thoughts before.
They will be friendly, since they will not know
the world without them, the tormented one.
They will speak softly. They will not be hard.

They are my night attendants; they, I know,
will count for me when all around my side
a tighter world comes on. How could they hide?
I'll open out tonight, and from outside
I'll call those corners in, whose breathing shows
that globes are simple, and that light can find
one dent beyond one valley at a time.

ANOTHER PREGNANT WOMAN REMEMBERS INCEST

Wailing, Cassandra came over the trees where we
lay, man and woman, and opened our eyes. We were
tired with the touch of the still-turning planets, and
tired with our dreams and the murders we knew (we had
kept generations of murder within us, and
now I was growing a murderer too).

Deep in my belly, the baby was quietly
turning away from the sound of the wail that grew
loud, as she crept in still closer to open her story, and
brushed her black hair near our ears, while her hands, with
whisper-through-agony silence, rested on me. I lay
listening hard to the sound of Cassandra, the sound of my

mother, the sound like the sea, while the knife went in
slowly and the old man shuddered, and no one was
left in the bathroom but me.

TONGUE OF LANGUAGE

Oh tongue of language, moving with your comb
past awful words to make the peace your home,
you are still my companion, though your love

still alters me, and ruins what I move
along to do, and kills me with you, love;
you love in words, you don't know what you move.

DUSK

When dusk and I are not the claims of dusk,
the hands of dusk, the chains, the open cuts,
the depth of dusk, I will not call them cuts.
Something flies by in speckles, in the dusk.
I'll call it land in waters that are light
and follow it, to drown instead in flesh,
as if I had an enemy in flesh,
since I will have no enemy in light.
Soon with the darkness all the arrows, charge
their hands, will hold me, and then open flowers
touch with their night-edged blossoms other flowers,
and dusk, now after me, with arrows charge
its loads of islands down from that high cave-
like walls-from-dripping night, and I am laved.

LESSON FROM A ROCK

I must hate all sad creatures who are weak
and talk to me; I know I hate their meek
self-sorry longing, and their stubborn creak.
They are the rocks wrapped sulky in wet moss,
crying to rocks on land, "perceive my loss!
The water blurs me and I live too far,
too shrinking from the size my sisters are"—
until the water, loud and laughing, sends
an open mouth down on her back, and mends
her life with roughened calls of light and thread,
and she lets the longing pattern seek her head,
while feet disturb the rocks exposed on land,
till night's wet touch makes all the sisters sand.

RECONCILIATION BREAD

Brown hills, on Milton's mind, were loaves and sent
out of my brain to feed him when he went.
He called me food and solace, and he strewed
me on his way among the hills. I grew (apace).

I called him carpenter. He took my bread
to carve along the grain, and grew a head
of highways, scattered up and gone
along the threads of earth I breathed upon.

Then I breathing sank and, sunk and breathing, drew
a carpenter to earth and his highway too.

NIGHT RAIN

With will the flicker of a candle flame
goes out though blown and in the iron house
the rain continues. This is such a house,
whose dripping galaxies untie dark time.
The drops that land are silent. In between,
the noise of growing flowers, like a scene
of gravity spent on the land between.

FAWNS

Mist that recovers everything and stains
the day with morning, rolling many rains

quietly past the open window panes
like no more reason, like a surrendered gain,

a child covering her eyes, a night in pain
surrendering into morning; you remain

mist over many mountains, valleys, lawns,
roofs, and at last my eyes: a mist of fawns.

AN IMAGINARY COMPANION

My blood was wise, my arms were weak, I was
a vessel from the inside. I could speak
alone, as if to water, that spoke back
beside me with no language, never stopped
to hear me, but continued, dark on black,
and if I'd been that way, I would not have stopped.
Two merciless companions, we were clocked
on our own time, as "water" and "free clock."
If it bit me, it bit me with the cold
and I ignored it—I bit back. So cold.
We have no hard companions. We are old
and warm as wild flowers, touch no ice,
have just a toe for one gold-rippled shallow,
and never make our conversations count
against the time that clocks me since I lost.

THE AGES' YEARS: A DIALOGUE

Windows are streaked. Sky must be autumn green.
The days' levels have lowered to a stream
where tigers seldom drink. "I know a team
of autumn revelers, whose hands are seen
in traces everywhere the nighttime's been."
Take me out of my room, where each new scene
has sulked across the ceiling in shadows.
Take me out to the autumn world, to roam
outside the legs of roaming, outside home.

HARVEST SEAM

It was November. I was not alone.
Send me your green, an endless pouring name
called from the skies that still had hands, that came
handed from clouds through tunnels. Any seam
was open, but the ear was mine, the crest
that climbed along the season till, the gleam
that slits November answering, I heard,
with scattered lips, in every pore, "Harvest."

"Harvest," it shattered. "Harvest. Don't come in.
Reaping on land comes on. Nothing comes in.
Stay out and harden fall and death and kin."
Still, like a midnight, I was not appalled.
I took the hands, and harvested, and fall,
a harvest, kept its nothing from my fall.

SUNDOWN

All through the forests, all the tired trails
he walked on through a mention of the rain
are filled with finds of fall, leaves down again,
and as he wonders, lit with sounding rain,
what edge or episode would bring it down,
a glorious sundown follows where the rain
and leaves have followed him, bringing it down.

Who is he? How did he talk sunset down
the way fall talks the leaves, and talk the leaves?
When no one saw him walking before the rain,
no one believed in him, but he was there,
killing the sunset, and now, in the rain,
we'll follow him; the sun is down again;
the rain is here; we're safe, and he is gone.

SHALLOW SKY

In the deep houses, cellars speak alone
till whisper-eucalyptus finds his home—
but stripped, and sodden, like a man gone by
and idly ruined—what once grew so high.

Now the deep houses are not the only gone.
His voice shows that more endings have been done.
And endings having done the endings, when
will endings come, and where can endings go?
Inheritors, we wait for it to show.

Not in the desperation of deep sky
or finitude of observation. I
have peace without that plenty. Shallow sky
unclench my fist, and sun lie on my eye
across my nose, and tell me how to die.

And it might come tomorrow. Many men
had their tomorrow yesterday. For them
I love a bomb; it ends me just like them.

Not in the desperation of deep sky
or finitude of observation. I
have peace without that plenty. Shallow sky
unclench my fist, and sun lie on my eye
across my nose, and tell me how to die.

CHILDLESS

And love looked out through other windows. We
were both inside me, looking, and along
the ocean love we felt the wind's big song
ruffling with thin branches, lying long
and down as leaves, then strong
we felt the wind pick up and go away.
We rocked alone and felt the housetop then,
and windows rocking, windows empty then.

Exultant wind, the song and life of men!
And windows rocking, windows empty then.

WRIST-BRACELET

An old bracelet, clawing its way through light,
has wombed out a morning episode: my niece
with hands, nephew with time, who speak an aunt
unpacified, who won't grow old, who won't
let out her hands through universe, release
her bracelet-wrist, unwind her wrinkling star—
and this black hole unwound, this skein of land
that man could walk on if I'd left my hand
unpeopled by its only grain of sand—
is still my hand, my episode, my man.

WINE-GLASS WOMAN

The early yellow dusk that pours from clouds
Strikes, as wine laces the trees above.
I sit alone here, holding up a glass
where wine's gold icy touch, the dust of men,
mists on the vineyards once all filled with men.

Men toil around me, while I raise the glass—
sinking, dripping, curling from its frame—
as if a sinking window held the glass,
or a dark mirror—an old looking-glass—
and I look between the mirror and the men.

LADY BUG

If any body turns and goes away,
I know it goes, as any branches go
away to grow out from their trunks, or birds
go any way on wings, on any cor-
ner of a handful-covered sky,
and hope for nothing, nothing. Nothing I
be anyone who touches. On an I,
I see a lady lying. I on I
On lady lay in spots of black, to die
before my body learns and minds to see,
whereon an arm of talking wants to be.
Our bodies needn't talk—there needn't be
a bridge for something of the old body.

A WREATH OF TIME

For Anne Bradstreet

Bursting with fruit, my lips have opened time
to duck into your valley, not behind
the walls of silence. I am not the line
you need to walk on or you need to see,
and I am in your heart. Courage for me
extends out to your hands. Your fingers see.

SHE THAT

The source of night is madness. I am she
that knows the way of madness. I am found
on edges of high capascades. I be
one of the edge of nutrients. Free me
and all the vanished kind find tapestry.

From The Encyclopedia of Scotland

INVOCATION

I saw the Muses winging through the air.
They said "Rust."
They said "Peace."
They said "Quiet."
They said "Peace,"
Like under water,
But the peace under water
Is not like sleep.
A howling comes. A call comes. Sheep. Sheep. Sheep.

First the rust. Then the quiet.
Then the noise. Then the hearing.
Then the mountains grow.
And then the sheep come flocking.
The moon is growing flinty now,"
They said with eighteen wings.
"The moon is growing flinty. Dusty. Speak.
You always stop when the ecstasy starts.
You are afraid of your instrument.
You are a-feared. You stop and cry,
"April in Paris, whom shall I turn to,
What shall I do with my heart?
April in Paris, whom shall I turn to?
Don't be too timid, don't be too strong
April in Paris, whom shall I turn to?
Youth is fleeting, to the rhythm beating
In your mind, oh my bridle, my bangle, my land,
My husband, my bridle, my bangle, my bride,
Let me pass!" And then you stop.

Since there's no talk, this seedless rain
Hath ruth nor reck, the touch of it,
Since there's no sound.

Rust. Quiet. Noise, hearing.
Moon growing, flint, dust, speak,
The mind's a knot, the mind's a furrow.
Open in the sun light, and heavy in the rain;
Since there's no talk, the touch of it
Hath ruth nor reck, this seedless rain,
Since there's no sound. The heart's a knot.

Let the pears bear on their backs,
The mushrooms grow out of the rain,
Let the pears bear out of the water,
The mushrooms grow up to the rain,
Green rain. Peppers, seeds, or pearls,
Those days when it comes right out of the ground
And makes itself as it falls or rises, not before.

Pears bear on their backs.
Mushrooms grow out of the water.
Pears bear out of the water,
Mushrooms grow up to the rain,
Green rain, like peppers, or seeds, or pearls,
Those days it comes right out of the ground
Or makes itself as it falls or rises, not before.

Trees come to life,
And us be trees
Us clouds of earth
Us gray dolphins.
Us clods of earth
Looking up the old gray stairs."

Then one of the Muses, Calliope hent,
Threw back her black hair and around the
wind-swept sea-drift gan to call
"Pessimistic!" "Dost thou not know?

What of a night devastated
She the lambs hight Casanova?
Here, in the glen?"

"No," I replied, and the lambs gat hence and spun
Driftings of homage around her heels high;
She returned, drifting, and the sense spun high

"Optimistic! "Surely thou know
That best of all possible betters the good
In this best of all possible cat worlds!"

"Thou knowest," I spied.
"The earth is awake." "Come here."
"Through all silence
you have been
AS A RAIN FROM OUT MY WINDOW.
You have sat delicately, rubbing the delicate rain
                around your heart."

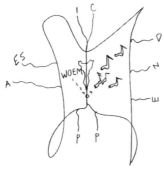

"Map of a Poem," illustration by
Annie Finch for the original edition
of *The Encyclopedia of Scotland*, 1982.

[1] Sixteen, to be exact.

[2] "If food is the object of migration why then did the song Sparrow leave us?"[0]

[6] Deleuze and Guattari, *Anti-Oedipus*

[1] A country song, I think.

[2] "Experiments in Aleatory Materialism", J. Miller, *The Old Singer*, 1980.

[3] Apparently an old Zen practice in certain schools.

[4] Manatee: some form of mermaid.[1]

[5] Frederick Jameson, unrecorded conversation with somebody else.

[6] An old jingle[2]

[7] Wallace Stevens, Sunday Morning.

[8] Samuel T. Coleridge, "Kubla Khan"

[20] "And can cat feel, being shod, my fair!"

[1] G.M. Hopkins, "God's Grandeur"

ONE, FROM "ROCKWOOD"

If I said you had a beautiful body, would you hold it against me?

When Daphne ran, leaving the god to stand,
holding his useless arrows in his hand,
did she mean really to flee from the huge and glorious hand
of Apollo Smintheus, leaving him really, baffled and
shining, to stand?

"I like it when the wind beats against me"
(drowning my head, blinding my ears)
"It makes me feel tangible, like a rock"

Walking along the shore by the garden,
gathering bits of jetsam,
saying, "It's thick, like a big pudding,"
about to go howling and sniffing like beasts on the trail,
being green green green but saying "yellow"
out of some little hole in the stomach.

Oh I love my love, he monitors everything I say,
he's got flanks, and he flicks, away, like a tail, through the water.
My love is blue, my love is a whale.
He's a blue dolphin. He never speaks,
nothing goes through him.
Oh my love's blue, my love's a seal,
my love's a manatee, he's an elephant,
oh I love my love, my love's a rhinoceros,
a fish, a fish, a huge huge moth!
Oh I love my love, he monitors everything I say!

Between the past and the prophet is the fall
Eve did it
fell us into beauteous night
fell us into burning, into drowning, into ghost
"As soon as you see a binareeee opposition, you know somethings
wrong."

We are sick, we have bodies.
Cats look like mice. Cats eat mice.
Cats eat mice. *But she never has.*

You, you, you coiled endlessly,
You, you, you stop and stare

Seven, I'm in Seven,
and my heart speaks so that I can hardly speak,
and the sixth sense is thinking, it's blue.
Seven, I'm in seven,
and I do not know much about sevens yet.
My deepest love however is between,
between the wide green banks of Hudson.
Between all the twos there are threes
and the fours. Twelve is the number of minutes, of signs,
of planets and minutes and months,
of minutes with fives but of months,
and there are four seasons, la la la la,
and there's only one

And the seventh is irony, red.

Eve came down to garden,
with humanity on her head.

Oh these are embers
Oh

Men are different they sleep
Our wonder to them is like horses'

Willful violence

the rope-ladder going down

Ghosts walk in our streets
on April
Fool's Eve and on All
Hallows Eve

"What's going on now?"
Come on, this is infinite!"
"I like blue watah, too!"

Oh, you, you, you coiled endlessly
You, you, you stop and stare

When Daphne ran, leaving the god to stand,
holding his useless arrows in his hand,
did she mean really to flee from the huge and glorious hand
of Apollo Smintheus, leaving him really baffled and shining to stand?

"I like it when the wind beats against me"
(drowning my head, blinding my ears)
"It makes me feel tangible, like a rock"
Or somebody beating
your head with a stick

Oh I love my love, my love monitors everything I say,
he's got flanks and he flicks, away, like a tail through the water.
My love is blue, my love is a whale.
He's a blue dolphin, he never speaks,
nothing goes through him.

Oh my love's blue, my love's a seal,
my love's a manatee, he's an elephant,
oh I love my love, my love's a rhinoceros,
a fish, a fish, a huge huge moth!
Oh I love my love, he monitors everything I say!

Walking along the shore by the garden,
gathering bits of jetsam,
saying, "It's thick, like a big pudding,"
about to go howling and sniffing like beasts on the trail.
Being red red red but saying "green"
out of some little hole in the stomach.

Oh these are embers
Oh

"As soon as you see a binareeee opposition, you know some-
thing's wrong." Between the past and the prophet
is the fall Eve did it
fell us into beauteous night
fell us into burning, into drowning, into ghost

We are sick, we have bodies, coffee beans grow on our hills,
we live in the chaff of the thresher of gardens,
bright with sinuous rills.
We're a field day.
We need a field theory to talk.

The air that strikes the surface of your eye,
of the squirrel's side eye as you wait in the garden
comes to you through water from TV. As you wait in the graveyard.
Cats look like squirrels.
Cats look like mice. Cats eat mice.
But she never has.
Cats eat mice. And she never has.

"Oh look how small they look, out in the boat!"

Oh Seven,
I'm in Seven,
and my heart speaks so that I can barely speak,
I do not know much about sevens yet.
My deepest love however is between.
Between the wide green banks of Hudson,
the mighty savages move. Between all the twos there are threes
and the fours. Twelve is the number of minutes, of signs,
of planets and minutes and months,
of minutes with fives but of months,
and there are four seasons, la la la la la,
and there's only one

It needs more definition.
Fish in the lake,
and planes in the sky.
So we don't just go trailing and sniffing like beasts on the howl.
It needs moh def in ignition
so we don't just go off like beasts on the prowl.
Howling and sniffing like creatures with tails.
Don't put your fingers in your mouth.
It isn't nice.

The white sheet is just plain ecstasy.
The way it blocks things from view,
and the peonies beaten down in the rain.

Here we are now
No I don't need a bag
I said
I don't
need a   gonly in the garden.
b   g
  a   g
     g

We have too many numbers for da da I just broke the bag
wood is attacking me it scratched my eyes
plastics like me it lets me open the grapefruit
juice bottle with my teeth

You know when everybody looks the same sometimes?
Sea water,
rain water.
You old dock.
I remember it well
maybe it was summer and they walked
into the dark kitchen and turned on the gas
The gas lamp? Or stove?
Stove, and made tea.

Everything I like about this place is because it reminds me of
something else
And the way you can see every square centimeter of space, because it's
so small

What a wind-fall!
You, the mountain!
We clip and clod all the lay of your land,
you swift horizon, thou!

What Is Ink in the water, on planets of rain.
Go down the old track and eat the apple back.
Eat the apple where it fell.
Eat the crab-apple wet in the grass.
Eat the crab-apple brown in the grass.
Eat the apple where it fell down.
Eat the apple on the ground.
Full of worms and red and brown.
Eat the apple every fall.
Eat it raw where it fell down
full of half-worms, red and brown.
Eat it in the fall near the road by your Aunt's house.
In our ways we have all been lucky
been luck row row, with luck in our wake,
in our rows lucky this way; of course there is a wake,
of course there is a fall, of course a rutted track,
a dusty road, a track, a wake, a furrow in the ground,
and only costing thou thou thou thou thou thou
thou sand names and not
much cost at that & all the cost at thou

Name any Victrola record
this is a wish fulfillment

Roses are red

The way you can see anything you want with your eyes closed.
Come come oh draw your face
the natural world
is coming to a close
come come oh draw your lungs
we won't need them where we're going I swear
it our lines will run in and w
e won't stay on the pages w
rof klim sa etihw eb lliw e

god is black,   s s s
lim sa etihw   s
k, for he bleeds black blood,   s
for he bleeds black blood,   s
for he bleeds green blood,   this
blood for our senses, the loss of our homes,   like
but he speaks   never
yellow breath   were
    for the hope   E
    of to come   V
        come   E
            come   D
                cNome
              A   come
            M   come
            A   come
          D   come
          A   come
        know   come
You   come

THE BODY OF THE THING,
FROM "FEEDING THE ADMIRAL'S PUSSYCAT"

An empty sheeting,
but that would be cheating,
ecstasy or not.

Well what would I want to give s s s ?

Rats. Mice.

There's something about last times
that's so silent, that covers the eyes,
that's so tender, that tenders thee forth,
that aches the lawns and covers the back of the garden
that dries the wood and opens the voices of doors that are
            calling us in as we leave you again
that dries the wood and loosens the voice of the porch

"Tell me a story," the old singer called,
tell me about the shadows of the green green grass
or something
From my trap I was so impatient
they were calling me from the blue singer
with wooden mock, tree mock they were mellowing
and devastating all the ruddy rocks I had dove off and worshipped
            and returned to, making a wind out of
            them, drowning my feet.

Heart's tooth I said humbly
the monastery orange
sings at the foot of the stairs

And they said you oaken stair-
case come out.

Whether I wood not
Whether I wood
oh that day, that day
I was not in the mood

Nothi g came rihgt
Nothing I was black tense, completely in the mood,
I passed water and it did no good to me
I loved all stone romantically
I carried lots of wood
I crusted over black, I imagined green death,
and all the wood was yellow and I rained
I COUNTED SHEEP.
And in that sleep
and in that sleep this too there is a dolphin
it came between my legs with back of grass
tense gray humorous skin
sat under my thighs like a sense
and I knew it myst be blue not red atall.
Blue single naïve
simply pulling in

Oh I hated each tread and each riser
Never hated anything so much.
Each blue trea. Each red riser. Each lichen-licking yellow metafour
                                    Up up up up
                            nwod nwod nwod nwoD
    Each rustling lickeling my crotch and each moth after all those sheep

First times are easy, a grand silver sadness loosens the mane, but
last times cover the fingers with soft new down, stretch us then
cup us in and Empty! Empty! Just in time to say goodbye . . .

Poems, 1979–1970

Sift and scald the ancient cups.

THE AUGUST PORCH

One afternoon:
I think I like it
better for cut browns
apples
lumber
than evening for the raveling of slats to emerald.

There's no gleam to the wicker.
Shadows might well
not be cast.

The trees are scanty
with the weight
of apples
they have finished.

But wisteria raises
its inchworm head and hunts
for the walls of this porch.

Something's waiting to run out on us.
The mist
and creak
of wines is due
when we run out of dusk.

SPELLS

From music, I bore
Some gold-stone fins,
but they sank away
through the waffled shallows.

From nature, I gleaned
Some hope of rice—
But it edged deep away
In sunk stone bowls.

So then I asked
For bowls and fins;
I asked for a hand
that could gather them back

into finning the shallows,
gilding, rounding.
I guessed me a hand
That could gather bowls open.

When I had asked
Whom I had guessed,
She sent my asking out.

Now over and over
she sends it back.
Over and over it answers me.

Over and over it answers, as she gives it,
in the speech of fins, and in the speech of bowls.

A DUSK SONG

Over the big bed in the small room
The flat shadow
Turned, thinning our walls
Insistently,
Turning and turning us closer and closer to salt wind
In from the sea.

I could sing a song about a long gone lover,
Cape Cod dusk, Cape Cod shadow;
I sang a song then about the Cape Cod shadow,
Over door and wall, over
Shoulder and shoulder.
Did I have a face and did it lie
In shadow
Turning and turning your glances away?

Once there was a song about the Cape Cod shadow;
I sang the song.
The flat shadow turned over our walls and brought the sea in.
The song kept turning.

IN CITIES, BE ALERT

You may hear that your heartbeat is uneven
and let new tension climb around your shoulders,
thinking you've found the trick for going mad.
But try to keep a grip on where you are.

Remember: all around you is pure city;
try to stay alert. On the wide streets,
so empty late at night, streaking in glass,
the color of an alley, or the fall

of a sideways flicker from a neon sign
may utterly and briefly disconcert you—
but as you go, you'll find that noise is worse.
Prepare for noise. But never scream. Even tensing

ears too far in advance can sharpen sirens,
and as for horns. . . . When you're back to
your normal rhythm after such encounters,

just try to stay alert. You'll never know
exactly who is coming up behind you,
but the sudden movement of pedestrians

will finally, of course, be what disarms you.

LIST

Crabs, seashells, white ants, cats,
A budding, a maple,
Iron, mint, wind starting.

Hills, birthing, seedling, root,
Rust, quiet, noise, hearing,
Crabs, seashells, white ants, cats.

Bay, webs, shells, foaling, milk,
Sap rising, fog, copper,
Iron, mint, wind starting.

Short thunder, open mouth,
Itch, billow, moon growing,
Crabs, seashells, white ants, cats.

Track, ripple, jolt, clay, touch,
A howling, a call, sheep,
Iron, mint, wind starting.

Air, rising, dying, leaf,
Beast, mouse, worm, what started,
Crabs, seashells, white ants, cats,
Iron, mint, wind starting.

A sunny afternoon; think of Vermeer.
Here is the apple, here the rounding side
of the blue pitcher. On the scrubbed wood just here,
she puts the pitcher down, so that the slide
of drops against its lip catches what light
there is for pitchers here this afternoon.
She does not really see the drops, or quite
attend the blue. A common thing. But soon
the tide will turn, and salty smells will rise
to circle in the street, and to her ears
will come the voices. Then doorways to her eyes,
then other days than this—afternoons, years.
She will stop to hold this moment near,
and drop the pitcher, and betray Vermeer.

COY MISTRESS

Sir, I am not a bird of prey:
a Lady does not seize the day.
I trust that brief Time will unfold
our youth, before he makes us old.
How could we two write lines of rhyme
were we not fond of numbered Time
and grateful to the vast and sweet
trials his days will make us meet?
The Grave's not just the body's curse;
no skeleton can pen a verse!
So while this numbered World we see,
let's sweeten Time with poetry,
and Time, in turn, may sweeten Love
and give us time our love to prove.
You've praised my eyes, forehead, breast:
you've all our lives to praise the rest.

WHEN DAPHNE RAN

When Daphne ran, leaving the god to stand,
Holding his useless arrows in his hand,
To stand, to run, and reach the forming tree
Just quickly enough to watch and touch the last
Dissolving into wood of the now steadfast
And rooted flesh, did she mean to flee
Really away from his huge and glorious hand,
Leaving him really, baffled and shining, to stand?
She had hated how he kicked his way through the wood,
Knowing a few of his low singing words would seduce
Her, calling his lust, letting his love loose
On her, big and imperious, crowding the trembling wood,
Till she suddenly ran, and he stopped for a second to stand.
The wood was still; he stared at his trembling hand.
She, still in the night, long after the god has gone,
Taking his tears, his lyre, his laurel wreath,
She, her mind growing vague already beneath
The layers of bark, vaguely remembering dawn,
Vaguely remembers: by dawn she'll forget the bright hand,
And the last way he touched her, before he left her to stand.

LUCID WAKING

Once I wanted the whole dawn not to let me
sleep. One morning, then, I awoke and watched as
waking woke me, came slipping up through half-light,
crying softly, a cat leaving her corner,
stretching, tall in the new gray air of morning,
raising paws much too high. She came slow-stepping
down the hallway to crouch, to call, to answer
through the door, making still and slow the dawning
once so bird-ridden—and the sun, the curtains—

SAPPHICS FOR PATIENCE

Look there—something rests on your hand and even
lingers, though the wind all around is asking
it to leave you. Passing the windy passage,
you have been chosen.

Seed. Like dust or thistle it sits so lightly
that your hand while holding the trust of silk gets
gentle. Seed like hope has come, making stillness.
Wish, in the quiet.

If I stood there—stopped by a windy passage—
staring at my hand—which is always open—
hopeful, maybe, not to compel you, I'd wish
only for patience.

ANOTHER RELUCTANCE

Chestnuts fell in the charred season,
Fell finally, finding room
In air to open their old cases
So they gleam out from the gold leaves,
In the dust now, where they dropped down.

I go watch them, waiting for winter,
Their husks open and holding on.
Those rusted rims are rigid-hard
And cling clean to the clear brown,

And the fall sun sinks soon,
And the day draws to its dark end,
and the feet give up the gray walk,
no longer lingering, light gone,
and I am here and do not go home.

Hollow gifts to cold children:
The chestnuts they hid in small caches
Have gone hollow, their gleam gone,
Their grain gone, and the children are home.

Line to line
the framings move
Window through window
through eyes.

Lake's water
moves through the house
Meets me in garden
all arched.

House is to
wall a window
with cup or a web
on sill.

Sill and pane
the framings move
Arched and glassed, they make
Complete.

FIRST POEM

The honest spirit
is bewildered
by the going of the night.
Bruised back by morning's light squares, she laments:

>   I've settled in a clan of waking ghosts.
>   There's no more solid thing for me than light.

But here the flick of evening opens
her who let stars' spider trails
run quick cold sticky errands through her night.

Day breaks into a pomegranate,
or some night of leaping patterns,
and she breaks to hear your words,
and now she's dialogue:

>   Attent me! Let the syntax crack!

>   My voice in an old tangle of synapse . . .

>   You will tug at the old strains daily

>   I'm a mirror, and a sieve

So sift and scald the ancient cups. Don't sleep.
Give your blanched filters back for homage.

CARIBOU KITCHEN

Most things have vanished
while we were talking
(the dents in a pitcher
gleam by the gas lamp),
but nothing is lost
(cups in far corners).
Arms still lean
over the table
(shadows on the oilcloth).

Performance Works, 1983–2010

You're the friend of the wild

"Calliope and the Sheep," illustration
by Annie Finch for the original edition
of *The Encyclopedia of Scotland*, 1982.

A CREATION STORY

(Excerpted and adapted from Sheba in Eden)

Dark stage with three trees stage left, one stage right. Perfectly still. A large egg is lying upstage center, lit from within. Stravinsky's Rite of Spring *begins to play as Snake enters from stage right and winds and twists around the stage. At 45 seconds, Snake exits stage left, as Cow enters stage right and walks slowly across the stage to exit stage left. At 1:14 seconds, two Birds fly [dance?] out from the same place, over the stage, and exit. Music ends at 1:53 seconds.*

Lights off, including light in egg. Beat.

VOICE [male?]:
Black, black of me, night of me,
if you were real—

ANOTHER VOICE [female?]:
if you were dark—

VOICE:
if you were cold—

ANOTHER VOICE:
if you were hollow,

VOICE:
if I were habit,

ANOTHER VOICE:
habit in a shell,
habit in the night—

Cow begins humming from offstage and ambles out from stage left, circling trees, chanting, as pale, warm lights fade slowly up upstage center, suggesting the tentative glow before dawn.

COW:
As I long walking
in my deep hand of leather
felt the edge of something holding
held folding by the corn

    Light fades slowly. Cow grazes slowly backward towards pool of light next to tree at stage right.

VOICE AND ANOTHER VOICE:
truth with the night,

    [Starlike lights appear [small white lights behind scrim?]]

VOICE:
light with the stars,

ANOTHER VOICE:
and rather something—

VOICE AND ANOTHER VOICE:
there is a thick crack

VOICE:
deeper than the deep black—

    Stars fade. Trees and voices make faint cricket noises.

COW [standing in pool of light]:
Deep roots I contorted
holding open as I could

    [A diffuse spotlight moves like a bird across stage.]

woke up with small light
held up the open
hand of the world

Blackout.
Cricket sounds fade to a sound like wind rustling in wheat that lasts for
three to four seconds.

ANOTHER VOICE:
The given is given.
What's seen has no light.
My gift has no rift.
My eyes have no sight.

COW

　　[coming to front of stage and tapping a rhythm with her hooves]:

And now it is dancing, dancing
as if it were planets holding

　　[White lights dance around cow and then settle on stage.]

all kinds of light;
there is sharp metal in my hoofs,
I tap out something from the ground,
I hear an element arriving,

　　[Cow stops tapping to listen.]

I call it dust and it will walk

ANOTHER VOICE:
Time will walk.

[Cow taps again as she exits stage left.]

[Lights on stage floor shake more and more quickly. The trees rustle their leaves. Rustling sound of wheat fast in microphone for ten seconds: feeling of the wind picking up to a more syncopated, energetic sound, as before a rain]. Then sudden cut to silence (as in middle of Beatles' song "A Day in the Life"). Lights dim.

VOICE:
The silent night had gone.
It backed back to the evening.
Then the turtle stopped its walking,
and the cow stopped its swaying,
then the birds stopped their dusk song.
Then the sun was going down,

ANOTHER VOICE:
then we came out of the egg.
Then we crouched inside and timed our hearts
together,

VOICE AND ANOTHER VOICE:
then we were gone.

> *Beat. Both voices exhale loudly into microphones, a full empty sound. Light on the egg.*

ANOTHER VOICE:
You, great sky,
you, all legs,
dark and light and cold, cold eggs,

VOICE:
Did you give life to the cow?

152

[Cow enters slowly stage left]

Will you give me countries now?
Watch this country with my eyes;
let some solid sights arise!

COW:
Hold your eyes, your raging eyes? Oh no.

[Chanting]

When I walk on the land, inside
the plains that ripple on my flank and side,
I'm like a grain of wheat.

[Stops chanting and faces audience]

I have no eyes.

> *Mirror ball lit for brief flashes as cow moves to downstage right. Birds enter stage left, dancing and calling around whole stage, then settle in the three trees as Queen of Sheba enters stage right, walks to center stage, and stands with cow, patting her.*

SHEBA:
The cow spoke truly when she said
her skin was just a grain of sand,
and though the ancient seeds can sprout,
though tombs alive a thousand years
can hold their gold paint and their wood,

> *["The Peaceable Kingdom" #2 is projected behind her. Melody from Schubert's Unfinished Symphony (1:15–1:58 seconds) starts very quietly.]*

though Cow's soft crying painted eyes
speak of the fields that have not died,
but bear their yields again for us, again,
I know her skin is just a grain of sand,
innumerable as clouds dispersed in rain.

> *Snake enters stage right and moves diagonally across stage through the trees,
> and stops at front stage left, where it remains till end. The birds are startled
> by this and fly out of trees toward upstage right, where they startle Cow. Cow
> runs and knocks into the egg, knocking it down. Cow looks at egg, stops, and
> walks carefully to the front of stage.*

COW [to audience]:
I am the cow that you believe.

> *Cow ambles over to stage left and comes gradually back to Queen of Sheba
> while Sheba speaks.*

> *[Lights down. Mirror ball lit. Queen of Sheba walks downstage right to
> stand in pool of light. Birds peck at the ground quietly, upstage right.]*

SHEBA:
Here on this continent whose leaves are falling,
whose edges are turning, whose colors are dropping,
here in this continent whose leaves are turning,
here are the animals.
Here are the hooves, here are the feet,
here are the tails that curl,
and here are the tails of the trees,
and the climate they make with their rotting leaves,
and here is the river that smells so strong,

> *[Cow comes back to stand slightly stage right, behind Sheba.]*

and keeps the rocks wet for so long,
and here is the air we made to breathe
the clover where the cow has trod,

[*She takes basket off her hip and starts to scatter glittering seeds.*]

the fruit the bird has found for seed,
the hay the lion and the horse can eat.
Here is the kingdom of peace and green,
of life and yellow, death and dream.

[*Birds move toward her and crouch low, facing Sheba as she feeds them seed.*]

We've made a forest, made leaves turn,
made the clouds in sunlight burn,
and food that grows, and time that rolls.
Here are the animals;
and bird is making further birds,
and time is making further time,
and fruit is seeding further fruit,
and here are the animals.

End

From *The Mermaid Tragedy*

ACT II
Interlude

> *Pele holding fire on a rocky platform at stage left towards the rear. Six*
> *women standing in a semicircle facing her, at stage right near the front. In*
> *the middle is Daphne, in darkness. Music starts slowly. Pele sways back and*
> *forth, swinging the light, which lights her robe. After a pause, the woman*
> *nearest the front begins to sway until she seems to fall out of her place and*
> *runs along the inside of the semicircle. The next follows, and the next, until*
> *the semicircle gradually disintegrates into a random circling from which*
> *the last woman to have left her place breaks free, running to circle Pele's*
> *platform clockwise, starting at the back of the stage. They all follow her in*
> *sequence and circle Pele four times in a gradually slowing procession. The*
> *women and Pele leave the stage. Green light on Daphne, who doesn't move,*
> *in a profusion of green leaves at the center of the stage.*

End of interlude

ACT II
Scene 1

> *Mermaid walks on stage, from stage right, in front of Daphne. She sits at*
> *the front of the stage facing front, meditatively. Daphne is still in the light.*

MERMAID
I don't know why I left when she offered me fire.
I don't know what I did; I don't know where I am.
All my friends are abandoned alone on their rock;
there's no one in their world left to help, without me.
I can never go back there, and they're all alone—

DAPHNE
Watching the murmuring edges they stay

MERMAID

I'm alone without friends; even Pele was kind,
and the trees were like friends, but I had to go on.

DAPHNE

opening doors in the forest you'd stay.

MERMAID

Would I stay? Could I stay? I'm not here. I'm too sad.
I had friends. They're alone. Without fire. Without me.

DAPHNE

But you'd stay here if you had a reason, like me.

MERMAID [turning slowly]

Is there really someone talking? I thought I was all alone.

DAPHNE

No, you're not here alone. I'm alone. You're with me.

> *Mermaid stands up and walks slowly and wonderingly towards her.*

MERMAID

Do you mean that I'm not here at all? That I'm free?

DAPHNE

Yes, you're free. As you step on the edge of my doubting, you're free.

> *Mermaid, who has been circling her and beginning to face away, begins to*
> *turn back toward her.*

DAPHNE

Don't come back, go away. You don't need to stay here.
I just won't think of you, and then you'll be out there,
and then you'll be as free as the others I know.

MERMAID

What do you mean, just as free as the others you know?
Who are these others, and why are they free?
I know that I'm not one of them; I'm not free.
I was chained to my home in the green living sea,
I was chained on the rock where I learned to walk free,
I was chained as I swam through the long, lying sea
that uses the stones that the land has set free;
now I'm chained in this forest, since you think of me?

    [Daphne rustles.]

What are you saying? Are you nodding or shaking?
Do you nod I'm not free? Do you shake that I'm free?

    [silence]

And why don't you talk, now you've listened to me?
Who are these others, and how are they free?
Who are they, Daphne? Why are they free?
I know I've been running in steps that aren't free, and my friends on
the island are less free than me, but they know that the goddess told
them what to do, are they freer than me? I don't know who told me—
Are you nodding? Why can't you talk now? Is it me?

    Enter Eve.

EVE

She can't talk now. The others are too near.

MERMAID

    [spinning quickly around]

Who are *you?* What are *you?* Why are *you* here?

158

EVE
I'm Eve, the worm. I'm here to comb her leaves—

She walks towards Daphne and begins to groom her.

MERMAID
Be careful—don't put tangles in the twigs!

She begins to help, separating the branches so Eve can comb them.

EVE
She's always quiet when there are others near,
so that's when I come here to take care of her.
She moves so wildly every time she talks.
Her passions are so green. She loses shape:
her branches touch, her leaves stick out, they bend
around each others' stems and then she shakes
her head again, and they all bend away
and bring the other stems with them and then
her leaves break like a cottage in the wind.

MERMAID
She is a wild person, then, I guess.

EVE
Only each time she talks. But other times,
like now, she's just as quiet as a tree.

MERMAID
Do you live in these woods? You seem to know her so well.

EVE
Don't you know? I thought everyone knew me.
I'm Eve, the worm. I've lived here for centuries.

MERMAID

No—you don't really look much like a worm—
What is this story? Why should I know you?
Why do you live here? Why should I have heard?

EVE

You've been far from the land—I see you have a tail—
that explains why you don't know of me.
But you don't need to know. I won't bother. I won't tell.
Why should you know how I got here? Help me pull.

> *They pull Daphne by her waist towards stage right, to the edge of the stage.*

Now! Now she'll talk. Talk to her. I'm all done. So goodbye!

> *Exit Eve.*

From *Marina Tsvetaeva: A Captive Spirit*

ACT III
Scene 3

> *Outside the office of the Council for the Writers Union in the tiny town of Chistopol. Marina is waiting anxiously with Lidiya.*

MARINA

My fate is being decided now. If they refuse me a residence permit for Chistopol, I will die. I feel sure they will refuse. I'll throw myself in the river Kama.

LIDIYA

The woman in gray looked up at me, slightly bending her head to one side. Her face was the same as the beret: gray. A delicate face but puffy.

MARINA

I hardly write any poems and this is why: I cannot limit myself to one poem—they come to me in families, in cycles, as a funnel or even a whirlpool in which I find myself, and consequently the problem is time.

LIDIYA

> *Sunken cheeks and eyes yellowish-green staring stubbornly. Her glance heavy, inquisitive. No smile at all, either on her lips or her eyes, and sentences without intonation.*

OFFICIAL

> *[emerging from the Council offices]*

Marina Tsvetaeva, your permit to reside in Chistopol has been approved. And it is also likely that you will be approved for the job as dishwasher in the Writers' Canteen.

LIDIYA

That's wonderful! Now you will be able to feed your son.

MARINA

[panicking]

Is it? Is it really worth looking for a room? Anyway, I won't find anything. If I find a room, they won't give me work. I won't have anything to live on.

LIDIYA

You are very lucky.

[They start walking.]

I'm glad Akhmatova is not in Chistopol. She would never have survived.

MARINA

[suspiciously]

Why?

LIDIYA

Because she would not have been able to cope with life here. You know that she cannot do anything practical at all. Even in city life, even in peacetime.

MARINA

[angry]

What!

LIDIYA
I saw the gray face at my side twitch.

MARINA

    [shouting furiously]

And you think that I — I can? Akhmatova cannot and I, you think I
can?

LIDIYA
I didn't mean that, no!
That's not what I meant, Marina!

AKHMATOVA AND MARINA
Timid, like a thief,
oh—not touching a soul!
I sat down at the absent table setting,
the uninvited, the seventh one.
There! I knocked over a glass!
And everything that thirsted to spill out—
all the salt from my eyes, all the blood from my wounds—
from the tablecloth onto the floor.
And there is no grave! There is no separation!
The spell is gone from the table, the house is awakened!
like death to a wedding feast,
I—life, came to supper.
I am no one: not a brother, not a son, not a husband,
not a friend—and still I reproach you:
you who set the table for six souls,
not seating me—at the edge.

CHORUS
Mother Marina, death follows your heart,
death walks with footsteps that echo your words.

Raise your head slowly, and listen again,
Mother Marina, Mother Marina.

Scene 4

> *The room in Yelabuga. Lidiya has been talking with Marina. She leaves*
> *the room and shuts the door.*

LIDIYA
Her poetry had no home.
Death came to the wedding feast.
Death came to the wedding feast.

CHORUS
It's time to take off the amber,
it's time to change the language
it's time to extinguish the lantern
above the door.

> *Marina is visible in silhouette writing a note.*

MUR
On the 8th of August 1941, I was evacuated to Yelabuga with my
mother Marina Ivanovna.

MARINA
Murlyga! Forgive me, but to go on would be worse.

MUR
We arrived on the 17th. On the 26th Marina went for two days to
Chistopol; she returned on the 28th to Yelabuga,

MARINA
I am gravely ill, this is not me anymore.

MUR

where she committed suicide on August 31. She was buried in the
Yelabuga cemetery.

MARINA

I love you passionately. Do understand that I could not live anymore.

MUR

It's time to take off the amber.
It's time to change the language.

MARINA

Tell Papa and Alya, if you ever see them, that I loved them to the last
moment and explain to them that I found myself in a trap.

MUR

It's time to take off the amber,
it's time to change the language
it's time to extinguish the lantern
above the door.

> *Mur leaves the stage. During the rest of the act, Marina is visible in
> silhouette placing the letter on a table, folding a garment and placing it on
> a bed, moving books off of a chair and placing them on the table next to the
> note, standing on the chair and hammering up a hook, tying a rope, and
> placing it around her neck.*

CHORUS

Mother Marina, you are a cool well,
dreaming of earth in the deep mouth of words.

MARINA

As if I'm free for a while from every worry
in meadows of sleep-giving grass!

CHORUS
and if here I've only an earthly name
it doesn't really matter

CHORUS
Mother Marina, you are a cool well,
dreaming of earth in the deep mouth of words . . .

MARINA
and if here I've only an earthly name
it doesn't really matter

CHORUS
Spin in your triumph, and turn in your pain,
Mother Marina . . .

MARINA
Your tears are like pearls in my crown.

CHORUS
Mother Marina, you are a cool well,
dreaming of earth in the deep mouth of words.
Spin in your triumph and turn in your pain,
Mother Marina, Mother Marina . . .

From *Among the Goddesses: An Epic Libretto in Seven Dreams*

ACT III (LIBRETTO VERSION)
Scene 1

> *Demeter's garden in Ohio: tall ripening tomatoes mixed with many herbs*
> *and flowers, near the side of a large barn. Demeter is picking peas and*
> *dropping them into a large metal bowl as Kouretes chant repeatedly, to the*
> *traditional tune: "Isis, Astarte, Diana, Hecate, Demeter, Kali—Inanna."*

Lily approaches silently and watches as Demeter sings to herself.

DEMETER
Long grass pushes up under the trees,
hyssop, bee balm, lavender, chicory,
mallow, johnny jump up, love in a mist,
coneflower, blackeyed susan, broccoli,
in my circular garden that curves from the earth . . .

LILY

> *[to herself and audience]*

Her hands are as wide, cool, and earth-stained
as mossy old rocks that a forest has patiently
grown up around, died around, fallen near.

DEMETER
spine in the planet, blood in the wind,
as I drop the peas in the aluminum bowl . . .
spine in the planet, blood in the wind . . .

KOURETES

> *[under the following conversation]*

spine in the planet, blood in the wind . . .

LILY
The arms of the planet are holding me alive.

DEMETER
I know everything old about Eve

LILY
Eve, the face of Demeter teaches me,

DEMETER
rose from fire as well as earth:

LILY AND DEMETER

   [standing to face each other]

Eve was the full gleam of light on the water.

DEMETER
Eve fell beside me, and rose and fell;
dark Eve, my own loss, my heartbeat, my sister,

LILY
Eve speaks to me often without loss or damage
in my heart from the place of the dead,
the place of the openings that I have found.

LILY AND DEMETER
Eve fell beside me, and rose and fell

   Lily crouches to help Demeter.

DEMETER

   [murmuring quietly as she works]

hyssop, bee balm, lavender, chicory,
mallow, johnny jump up, love in a mist,
coneflower, blackeyed susan, broccoli,
in my circular garden that curves from the earth . . .

KOURETES
Here is the mother who'd watched her own daughter
given away, and ruined the earth,
who now put out leaves, and nurtured the earth,

DEMETER

    [murmuring quietly in the background]

Caves run hollow until I can fill them
with silent energies seeding new quiet . . .

    Lily stands up suddenly at the word "crystals" and speaks as Demeter
    continues murmuring.

DEMETER
. . . crystals to form, and roots to come down
into their veins; with water that pushes.
with stems reaching, trunks reaching, leaves setting bone.

LILY

    [forcefully]

I'd been invaded; the baby was not mine.
Why should I carry it?

KOURETES
Coneflowers blew
fuschia and silent, as if there was laughter,

LILY
from the breeze that was suddenly simpler,
as if there could once more be joy. It has been
months since I'd felt like myself, like Lily;
months since my life has moved for me.

DEMETER

[finishing picking and rising, stretching]

When my darling Persephone was young,
she cried every time I pulled weeds. It was hard
to see that. It's hard to let go. We need to.

She puts her arm around Lily. They go inside the barn together.

KOURETES
silent energies seeding new quiet
crystals to form, and roots to come down
into their veins; with water that pushes.
with stems reaching, trunks reaching, leaves setting . . .

Scene 2

*A rainy highway, with a small house in the distance. If possible the Serpent
Mound, an ancient earthwork in the shape of a long snake, is visible.
Kouretes at the side of the stage.*

*Lily steps off a bus, lifts her coat up to cover her head, and begins to walk up
the road.*

KOURETES
The other heart has begun its beating
The other heart has begun its beating
in the rich cave, the long silence

LILY

[as she walks]

The other heart has begun its beating
in the rich cave, the long silence
the hoping morning that was my womb.

KOURETES
The other heart has begun its beating
The other heart has begun its beating

LILY
Through my belly run knife-hard images
to my body and to my heart.
The hate that touched me on the mountain
is still thriving, making a silence

KOURETES
is still thriving, making a silence

LILY
deep in me still, a yielding mine,
where my own thoughts cannot find a foothold
but plummet, hopeless, down in my body,
absorbed by its power. I stay quiet.
Houses start to thin out around me.

KOURETES
Houses start to thin out around me.
Night fills the horizon's undulations,
branching out in darkening trees.

LILY
We are approaching the Serpent Mound,

KOURETES
We are approaching the Serpent Mound
We are approaching the Serpent Mound
We are approaching the Serpent Mound

LILY
I walk cautiously, knowing my belly
full of wide wings, night, and starlight.

> [She approaches the house. A flame shines through a window.]

I can see her, sitting, sewing
on a huge tapestry.

> Lily knocks

KOURETES
She stands up slowly.
She puts the tapestry down on the table.
We see in its folds a glimpse of creation,
animals, planets, mountains, and trees,
embroidered thick with contrasts and colors,
on a background as warm as blood.

> The door opens. Kali appears there, looks around blankly, and shuts the door.

> After a moment of silence, Lily runs forward angrily and pounds on the door.

From *Wolf Song*

ACT II
Scene 1

*Music stops. A wolf trail at the front of the stage. Sound of Wolf Howls.
In silence, nine Wolf Puppets move along the trail.*

DEER CHORUS

[song starting softly and gradually mounting in speed and exuberance]

The wolf is coming back, the wolf is coming back!
The wolf makes us strong, the wolf makes us strong!
We are the deer that the wolf makes strong,
We toss our antlers and we move along,
When the wolf is here we let some trees alone,
We let the brush grow thick and animals come,
We let the fish and birds and the butterflies thrive
We help the whole planet come alive!
The wolf is coming back, the wolf is coming back!
The wolf makes us strong, the wolf makes us strong!
The wolf heals our forest, the wolf heals the trees,
The wolf fills the world with the balance of ease . . .

The last Wolf Puppets disappear down the trail.

DEER CHORUS SOLOIST

[chanting as in plainsong]

The wolf-path is long and respectful,
trodden next to the forest.
Centuries of wolf feet have trodden
the path next to the forest,
Lined with scat and bones,
with antlers and carcasses

going back to the earth,
to our home in the earth . . .
And the Blackfeet say that the Milky Way
Is the wolf trail to heaven
The Blackfeet say that the Milky Way
Is the wolf trail to heaven
Their strong fast feet tread it,
Their spirits have fed it,
the path next to the forest.

ACT II
Scene 4

Red is walking far off in the forest.

RED
With a remembered sound
Faint as empty morning
Waiting with hollow wings
Till the far bird sings . . .

Gradually, the Deer Chorus surround her.

RED
Who comes down through the fields,
From the ridge where the foot pads
Walk and follow the trail,
As they've done for long decades?

DEER CHORUS

[dancing around her as they sing, throughout this scene]

The wolf is coming back, the wolf is coming back!
The wolf makes us strong, the wolf makes us strong!

RED
Who comes gray through the tawny
Wiry brush of the meadow,
Takes the elk in the field,
Breaks bones with bones, like a linking?

DEER CHORUS
The wolf makes us strong, the wolf makes us strong!
The wolf heals our forest, the wolf heals the trees,
The wolf fills the world with the balance of ease . . .

FENRUS

    [from offstage]

Wolf! Wolf! Wolf!

    The Deer Chorus fade back into the trees, still slightly visible.

RED

    [following the sound to edge of the trees at stage right]

Fenrus, what are you up to? What do you mean, Wolf?

FENRUS

    [more quietly, appearing]

Wolf!

RED
Did you really see a wolf?

FENRUS

Oh yes! My name is Fenrus, and that means Wolf, and I did see a wolf!
And I'm going to tell my dad—and he's going to come and kill it—just
like he did last time! The time he let you out of the wolf's belly and
you came back to life and ran away!

They sing a duet, intertwining their songs and voices.

FENRUS

[in duet with Red]

Pa's coming back to kill it.
Now my Pa will come kill it.
Eye and nose and fur and skin
Now he'll save us all again
Just like he did before
Eye and nose and fur and skin
It answers when he comes again
The wolf will answer to his gun
Eye and nose and fur and skin
Now he'll save us all again
Just like he did before
Eye and nose and fur and skin
Just like he did before

RED

[in duet with Fenrus]

Eye and nose and fur and skin
We can make the wolf begin
I sing in the heart, I sing in the voice,
I sing the bones that have no choice
Eye and nose and fur and skin

We can make the wolf begin
It's time to move and come alive
The bones will need you to survive
Eye and nose and fur and skin
We can make the wolf begin

The Deer Chorus fade away completely.

FROM ACT III
Scene 2

> *La Loba's clearing. Spring. Before dawn. Shadow and increasing light play softly through the new leaves. La Loba is alone, singing over the bones.*

LA LOBA

> *[humming the bone-song]*

Hmmm, hmmmm. Hmmm, hmmmm . . .

> *Dawn and fog come up slowly.*

LA LOBA

> *[barely visible through the fog]*

Eye and nose and fur and skin
We can make the wolf begin
I sing in the heart, I sing in the voice,
I sing the bones that have no choice . . .

> *Deer Chorus appear like shadows, dance briefly around her, move back into trees.*

LA LOBA
Eye and nose and fur and skin
We can make the wolf begin

DEER CHORUS
And so many days of winter went by
And spring came for La Loba
Spring came for the bone-singer
Spring came for the bones . . .

   La Loba gets up and dances.

LA LOBA AND DEER CHORUS
It's time to move and come alive
The bones will need you to survive
Eye and nose and fur and skin
We can make the wolf begin

LA LOBA
Sometimes I think I feel a stirring in the bones
I know I am getting close to moving these bones!

   *The Wolf Puppets who were on the trail at the beginning of Act II move
   across the stage again. Then a group of Deer Chorus dancers appear at the
   edge of the forest. They are carrying the big mask of the Wolf from Act I.
   They move to the edge of the clearing and put it down. Red crawls out from
   inside the jaws.*

LA LOBA

   [hugging Red]

Red???! Red! Inside the wolf! What happened, honey? Are you all
right?

RED

[hardly able to talk]

Grannie, Grannie! . . . so beautiful!

[Red in unison with La Loba]

It was so beautiful!

LA LOBA

[hugging Red again]

Tell me!

RED

It was the wolves, Grannie! I—I—was so tired and I got lost—and
they were so warm—their fur—there was one—a mother—she let me
stay with her babies—they saved my life!

LA LOBA

[singing quietly as Red is talking]

Coming out of the forests, gray form emerging
Soft fur emerging like flowers
Here is your pelt
Your tail electric with life
Flying wild in my hand
Brush made of goddess
You're the friend of the wild
Alive in your death
You fill my life still
Your bones are waiting for me now,

They carry me to life.
By all the power in my bones,
I'll answer you with life.

[She is still holding Red tight, but speaks to the forest]

Thank you!

RED
Grannie, now I really understand! I know why you are always singing
that old bone-song! Now I know why you need to bring the wolf alive
again!

LA LOBA
Red!

RED
The floor of the forest is stirring,
The hearts of their feet are moving,

LA LOBA
The hearts of their feet are moving,
They come out of the forests, their gray forms emerging
From gray dawns, like ashes
Soft fur emerging like flowers . . .

Lights go on and off as they sing and Fenrus continues to dance around
them. Fenrus is joined by the Deer Chorus. He wears a deer headdress like
theirs as they dance together. The Hunter, on the ground under a tree in the
same place Fenrus was at the beginning of the play, watches intently as if
having a dream.

RED AND LA LOBA

[singing, duet]

We sing in the heart, we sing in the voice,
We sing the bones that have no choice
It's time to move and come alive
And the Blackfeet say that the Milky Way
Is the wolf trail to heaven
The Blackfeet say that the Milky Way
Is the wolf trail to heaven
Their strong fast feet tread it,
Their spirits have fed it,
the path next to the forest,
Eye and nose and fur and skin
It's time to make the wolf begin
Eye and nose and fur and skin
It's time to make the wolf begin.

Several of the Deer Chorus invite the audience to sing along with this chant. At the climax of the chant and dance, the lights change again and a magnificent wolf-mask, red and green and a touch of yellow, appears covered with stylized glittering and patterns.

RED

[coming to stage front and singing with increasing excitement as the others continue their songs]

With a remembered sound
Faint as empty morning
Waiting with hollow wings
Till the far bird sings . . .

Sound of a bird, loud, as the Wolf Dancers slowly appear and surround Red.

LA LOBA

[gasping]

There she is—the Wolf!

Red puts on the wolf mask, becoming a wolf, and joins the rest of the wolf pack as they run off through the forest.

End

Translations, 1978–2010

We need
All the hollows

THE SEAFARER

From the Anglo-Saxon, c. A.D. 550–950

I keep the track
I'll tell of trials,
hard days,
I have borne
held on ships
Awful sea-waves
narrowed watches
and the ship beat cliffs.

were my feet, bound in fros
with chains of cold,
my ocean-weary mood.
whom fair things
how, care-worn wretch,
and wintered an exile's
shorn of kin,
hung with icicles.

There I heard only
ice-cold wave,
of swans for a game,
and curlew's song
mew's singing
Storms beat the stone cliffs;
icy-feathered.
could help my heart,
And they hardly know,
by staying in towns,
lustful and flushed,
was forced to stay out

of a song true of me:
struggling times,
and how I endured.
such bitter cares,
whole houses of cares.
tossed where I kept
on the stern at night

Thronged in cold
bound in thoughtt
while hunger slit
They do not know,
befall on land,
I stayed at sea
icy tracks,

Hail-showers flew.

the whirring sea,
or else the call
gannet's laughter
for human laughter,
for mead to drink.
the tern answered,
No strong kinfolk
which hollowness held.
who have life's joy
they of few hardships,
how often I, weary,
on the salty sea.

Night's shadow darkened,
ground bound by frost;
coldest corn . . .

a thought in my heart
the high waves,
my heart's need
my spirit out
seeking only
And there is no person
nor so good in gifts,
nor so eager in acts,
So as not to sorrow
about what Heaven
Our minds are not
nor on joy in love,
nor on anything else—
We are always longing,

Groves take blossom,
fields brighten;
then all urges
to journey out,
to move far
And the cuckoo urges,
the guard of summer
a hoard of sorrow.
the soft easy folks,
who lay these wide

Now my heart turns
my mood moves
it turns wide, high over whale-paths—

snow from the north,
hail fell on earth,

And now! there beats
that I should try
the salty tossing;
always urges
away from here,
another place.
so bold on the earth,
nor so quick in youth,
nor with friends so kind,
    at sea always,
might finally bring.
on harping, nor on rings,
nor on bliss in this world,
but on that tossing.
we who move over water . . .

towns are adorned,
the world moves on;
the pressing mood
in those who crave
on flood ways.
calling sad;
sings, boding
They do not know,
what some undergo
exile's tracks . . .

high over hemming breast,
out with the sea-flood,

sweeps of the earth—
winged and eager —
whets for whale-ways
the stretch of the seas . . .

the delights of Heaven,
loaned us on land.
that earth's ways
One of three things
down to doubt
Sick or old
doomed and wrecked,
For each noble, therefore,
of after-speakers—

So here let us work,
good deeds on earth
brave deeds
so all our children
and our praise then
for long ages,
delight of that host . . .

carrying the pomp
now quiet are
the gold-givers
with mighty deeds
and lives known

All that host has fallen.
the worst are still here
busily share in it.

and swoops back to me
the hungry one yells,
my breast resistlessly,

and to me they are hotter,
than this dead life
I do not believe
stand eternal for Heaven.
brings each noble servant,
before the last day.
or hated by a sword,
our lives are wrenched.
the praise of the living,
word-tracks—are best . . .

before we have to go,
against demons' evil,
to the harm of the devil,
will extol us,
live with the angels
eternal life's glory,

Days have departed,
of earth's countries;
the crowns and caesars
who've gone before,
made among themselves,
for the noblest renown . . .

Delights have faded;
and they hold the world,

Glory is bowed;
earth's dignity ages and ends,
as each of us does throughout our world.

Age gains on us, our faces pale,
grizzle-headed we grieve; our friends have gone,
royal children changed into earth.
Nor can the house of flesh, when life has failed us so,
taste the sweet nor feel the sore
nor stir a hand nor hold a thought.

And though on the graves of our great dead
we strew gold, bury with death
various gifts, they do not go along;
nor may the soul that is full of sin
find strength in treasure from the terror of Heaven,
if we've hoarded before, while we dwelled here.

Great is the terror of the Measurer, and the world moves aside;
The Measurer made the massive ground,
the sweeps of earth, the arching sky.
They are foolish who do not dread the Maker; death comes to them unforeseen.

They are blessed who live in gentle mood; grace comes to them from heaven.

The Measurer marks in us that mood, so we'll believe in the Measuring strength.

We should steer strong moods and hold them steady,
wise in pledges, pure in ways.
Each person should in measure hold
love towards beloved and malice towards foes,
even though we see, singed with fire
and with anger, the burning death

of a friend we love.
the Measurer mightier,

Let us think
and then consider
and then try always
on that eternal
where life is held
bliss in the Heavens.
that we've been made worthy—
always,

Fate is stronger,
than any of our ideas.

where our home is
how we came here,
so we can enter
easiness
in the love of the Maker,
Let the Sacred One be thanked,
by the world's Elder,
for all time.
         So Must It Be.

SONNET 2 [HANDSOME BROWN EYES]
By Louise Labé

Ah handsome brown eyes—ah eyes that turn away—
ah burning sighs; ah tears that stretch so far;
ah night I vainly wait for, without a star;
ah luminous and vainly returning day—
oh sad complaints; oh love's stubborn play;
oh lost hours; oh wasted pain and war;
oh thousand deaths, each in a tightened snare;
oh sullen evils that design against my way.
Ah laugh, ah forehead, hair, arm, hand, and finger,
ah plaintive lute, viola, bow, and singer—
so many flames to engulf one single woman!
I despair of you; you carry so many fires
to touch my secret places and desires,
but not one spark flies back, to make you human.

SONNET 5 [BRIGHT VENUS]
By Louise Labé

Listen, bright Venus—errant in the air!
Do you hear this clear voice moving, as I sing
to your face, shining so high above everything,
about my long labor and my exhausting care?
My eyes grow softer with this night's long stare,
and as you look you'll see much, much more weeping.
More tears will dampen my bed, with your eyes watching,
though they trouble the sight of witnesses so rare.
Humans are weary now. Their spirits sleep
in the gentle hold of rest that pulls them deep.
But my pain will last as long as the sky is bright,
and when, almost completely broken, I
am pulled to my tear-wet bed, I'll plead and cry
with hurt that will hold me through the whole long night.

SONNET 13 [THE IVY AND THE TREE]
By Louise Labé

Oh, if I were taken to that handsome breast
and ravished by him for whom I seem to die,
if I could live with him through all of my
short days, free of the envy of the rest;
if, clinging to me, he'd say, "We're so blessed,
dear Love; let's be contented just to lie
together, proving to flood and stormy sky
how life can never break our close caress"—
if I could tighten my arms around him, cling
as ivy surrounds a tree with its circling,
then death would be welcome to envy and destroy.
And if then he'd give me another thirsty kiss—
till my spirit flew away through his sweet lips—
I would die instead of live, and with more joy.

SONNET 14 [THE POINT OF DEATH]
By Louise Labé

While my eyes can still pour out fountains of tears,
mourning our shared hours, gone now, so long gone;
while my slow sighs and sobs can still bemoan
the loss of you in a voice someone might hear;
while my hands can still caress this lute to clear
praises for any grace you might have shown,
and while my spirit remembers to bend alone
on you, on nothing that's outside your sphere—
I'll never want to reach the point of death!
Though when my eyes grow dry and this voicing breath
is broken and my hand is powerless,
and when my spirit takes its mortal flight,
beating with no more signs of love—yes, then, I'll press
for death to come cover my clearest day with night.

SONNET 16 [IMPOTENCE]
By Louise Labé

After a time in which thunder and hail
have beaten the mountains—the Caucasian height—
a fine day comes, and they're clothed again in light.
When Phoebus has covered the land with his circling trail,
he dives to the ocean again, and his sister, pale
with her pointed crown, moves back into our sight.
When the Parthian warrior has spent some time in the fight,
he loosens his bow and turns from his travail.
When I saw you plaintive once, I consoled you, though
that provoked my fire, which was burning slow.
But now that you have given me your embrace
and I am just at the point where you wanted me,
you have quenched your own flame in some watery place;
now it's colder than my own could ever be.

SONNET 18 [KISS ME AGAIN]
By Louise Labé

Kiss me again, rekiss me, and then kiss
me again, with your richest, most succulent
kiss; then adore me with another kiss, meant
to steam out fourfold the very hottest hiss
from my love-hot coals. Do I hear you moaning? This
is my plan to soothe you: ten more kisses, sent
just for your pleasure. Then, both sweetly bent
on love, we'll enter joy through doubleness,
and we'll each have two loving lives to tend:
one in our single self, one in our friend.
I'll tell you something honest now, my Love:
it's very bad for me to live apart.
There's no way I can have a happy heart
without some place outside myself to move.

SONNET 19 [A MEETING WITH DIANA]
By Louise Labé

Diana, standing in the clearing of a wood
after she had hunted her prey and shot it down,
breathed deep. Her nymphs had woven a green crown.
I walked, as I often do, in a distracted mood,
not thinking—when I heard a voice, subdued
and quiet, call, "Astonished nymph, don't frown;
have you lost your way to Diana's sacred ground?"
Since I had no quiver, no arrows, it pursued,
"Dear friend, who were you meeting with today?
Who has taken your bow and arrows away?"
I said, "I found an enemy on the path,
and hurled my arrows at him, but in vain—
and then my bow— but he picked them up in wrath,
and my arrows shot back a hundred kinds of pain."

SONNET 21 [LOVE FORCES MY JUDGMENT]
By Louise Labé

What height makes a man earn the most admiration?
What weight? Which hair? What color of skin and face?
Which eyes brim fullest with the honeyed grace
that spurs the most incurable sensation?
Which song brings man's voice to the highest glorification,
its sadness penetrating the deepest place?
On whose voice does a lute leave the sweetest trace?
Which nature best feels love's warm palpitation?
I wouldn't want to claim that I know best,
since Love forces my judgment. But nonetheless,
There's something I do know. I know I'm sure
that all the beauty I could choose to explore,
And all the art that might improve on Nature,
could never increase this desire—not one bit more.

SONNET 23 [THE TANGLE]
By Louise Labé

What good is it how well, alas, you sang
those long-ago praises to my rich gold hair,
or told me how my gorgeous eyes compared
to suns from which Love's brightest arrows sprang,
tormenting you again with each sharp new pang?
Oh tears, that dry so quickly in the air;
oh Death, on which you promised you would swear
your love—and where your solemn vows still hang—
(or was the aim of your deceitful malice
to enslave me, while seeming to be in my service?)
This time, oh love, I know you'll pardon me
this tangle of all my anger and grief entwined;
since I know for sure, wherever you may be,
you endure your martyrdom, as I do mine.

THE WHITE BIRD
By Anna Akhmatova

So worried about me, so jealous, so tender—
As steady as God's sun, as warm as Love's breath—
he wanted no songs of the past I remembered.
He took my white bird, and he put it to death.

At sunset, he found me in my own front room.
"Now love me, and laugh, and write poems," he said.
So I dug a grave in the old alder's gloom,
Behind the round well, for my happy, bright bird.

I promised him I wouldn't cry any more;
The heart in my chest is as heavy as stone,
And everywhere, always, it seems that I hear
The tender, sweet voice of the one who is gone.

Translated with George Kline

CLEOPATRA
By Anna Akhmatova

> *I am air and fire . . .*
> —*Shakespeare*

> *Alexandria's palaces*
> *Were covered with sweet shade.*
> —*Pushkin*

Already, she's kissed him, her Antony, on his warm dead lips.
Already, she's kneeled down in front of Augustus and cried.
And now she's betrayed by the servants: victorious trumpets
sound under the Eagle of Rome, and the darkness spreads wide.
The last of her beauty's tall conquests comes in, his voice grave;
his stammering whisper enfolds her as he bends to say,
"They'll lead you before him in the Triumph—you, like a slave . . ."
Her throat, like the neck of a swan, holds its tranquil sway.

Tomorrow, the children in chains. And so little remaining
for her in the world; just to banter again with this man,
then take the black snake in a gesture like pity, and bring
it close to her rich breast at last, with her indifferent hand.

Translated with George Kline

LOT'S WIFE
By Anna Akhmatova

But his wife looked back from behind him, and she became a pillar of salt.
—*Genesis 19:25–26*

The righteous man followed where God's angel guide
shone on through black mountains, imposing and bright—
but pain tore his wife's breast. It turned her aside
and said, "Look again! There is time for one sight
Of towers, and Sodom's red halls, and the place
Where you sang in the courtyard or wove on your loom
By windows now empty—where you knew the embrace
Of love with your husband—where birth filled the room—."
She looked. And the sight was more bitter than pain.
It shut up her eyes so she saw nothing more;
She shimmered to salt; her feet moved in vain,
Deep rooted at last in the place she died for.

Who weeps for her now? Who can care for the fate
Of someone like that—a mere unhappy wife?
My heart will remember. I carry the weight
Of one who looked back, though it cost her her life.

Translated with George Kline

THIRST
By Andrée Chedid

Is it the absence of thirst
That locks up our words?
Is it the dry text
That reduces us?
Is it emptiness
That undermines our song?

IN PRAISE OF EMPTINESS
By Andrée Chedid

We need
The empty
To find
The full
So that the dream
Unfolds
So that the breath
Takes in

So that the fruit
Sprouts
We need
All the hollows

And the want.

A FRAGMENT OF SAPPHO

It is not appropriate, in a household
Given to the Muses. Those lamentations
Do not belong here.

ACKNOWLEDGMENTS

My poetry has been blessed by supportive and encouraging people from all parts of my life for as long as I can remember: family members, neighbors, teachers, librarians, readers, friends, students, writers, poets, fans, acquaintances, chance encounters, healers, comrades, editors, publishers . . . I could never even begin to thank everyone here, but it is my pleasure to add a few special acknowledgments that stand in for many more: to Jane Clow, Cara Forte, Jen Fox, Deborah Tallerico, and all my circles and covens for keeping me connected to the Muse; to teachers far too many to name, but especially Marie Borroff, Penelope Laurans, Ntozake Shange, and Diane Wood Middlebrook; to Jennifer Lunden, Jan Perkins, Dick Schoenbrun, and the many talented and compassionate healers who helped me uncover the path to these poems; to Wendy Ashley and Gretchen Lawlor and seers who illuminated the way; to Ann Bogart, Stefania deKennessey, Deborah Drattell, Cait Johnson, Assunta Kent, Laura Manning, Libby Marcus, Mihku Paul, Bruce Rockwell, Lisa Siders, and other artists of music, painting, photography, sculpture, architecture, book arts, puppetry, theater, and dance who inspired so much of this poetry by sharing the gift of creative collaboration; to colleagues in poetry far, far, far too many to name, but especially Kazim Ali, Cynthia Hogue, Carolyn Kizer, Stephen Motika, Molly Peacock, and Sonia Sanchez, each of whom believed in my work at a time when it kept me going; to Dabney Finch and Tara Wegryn and the young soldier on the Delta flight, for reminding me that my poems can and do reach people anywhere; to Lee Bricetti, Alice Quinn, and other inspiring supporters of poetry; to Alix Baer Bacon, Erica Bogin, Leslie France, Kristen Ghodsee, Tom Glushko, Gabrielle Jonas, Tamara Razi, Marie Truscott, and the others who helped me never feel alone; to Colleen Donovan and all the friends and neighbors who helped provide a village for my children during the years many of these poems were written; to my remarkable clans of origin, Finch, Ridley, Crane, Baker, Hughan, West, Donaldson, and Rockwell, for their passionate involvement and commitment to art, poetry, and spirit, many generations deep—especially my father Roy Finch, perpetually eager to talk poetry, and my mother Margaret Rockwell Finch, my first and deepest poetic model; to Robin Talbot, Heather Magaw, and all at University of Southern Maine and Stonecoast MFA for their humor and patience as I balance all my jobs; to my amazing children Julian and Althea, for inspiring me so deeply and for a million rich and clear conversations on poetic topics big and small; and to Patricia Monaghan and Michael McDermott for tender and brilliant matronage and patronage of the highest creative order.

Finally I would like to thank Glen Brand for his caring husbandry of my life, my poetry, and my heart. Since 1985, Glen has encouraged me in despair, comforted me in rejection, listened to me in loneliness, and celebrated with me in triumph; he has shared poetry aloud, endured sleep broken by flashlights and computer screens, brought me a well-timed pen and notebook on more than one occasion, and helped me through the difficult and challenging logistics of a poetic career with a ready sense of humor, brilliant and level-headed insights, and unwavering support. He has also, as this book will attest, inspired many love poems. I could never have asked for a more magnificent mate to accompany me on the path of poetry, and this book would not be itself without him.

The poems in this volume first appeared in the following journals and collections, to the editors of which I render grateful acknowledgment:

"Homebirth" first appeared in *Prairie Schooner*. "Abortion Spell" first appeared as "The Kiss: A Rhyme for Blood and Peace" in *Women's Studies Quarterly*. "Stone and Cloth and Paper" first appeared in print as "Rainy Day Room" in *Cerise Press*. "Frost's Grave" first appeared in *Visiting Frost: Poets Inspired by the Life and Work of Robert Frost*. "Tarot: The Magician Card" first appeared in *Yale Review* and subsequently in *The Wolf* (U.K.). "Keys" first appeared in *The American Scholar*. "Beach of Edges" first appeared in *Villanelles*. "Earth Day" first appeared on the *Friends of Ballona Wetlands* website and was circulated by the Sierra Club as a "Daily Ray of Hope." "Goddess" appeared in *Walking between the Stars*. "Speak Softly" appeared as "The Native American Birds" in *Kansas Quarterly*. "A Small Sound in the Dark Woods" appeared in *Ars Interpres* (Stockholm). "Spells" appeared as "Liturgy" in *Yale Lit* and in *The Body of Poetry: Essays on Women, Form, and the Poetic Self*.

Thanks to the editors of the following journals, which published some of the Lost Poems: *Black Clock*: "Dusk"; *Oranges & Sardines*: "Song of the Sorry Side"; *Smartish Pace*: "Lesson from a Rock" and "Now in November"; *Fulcrum*: "Reconciliaton Bread"; *Jacket*: "Night Rain" and "She That"; *Ekleksographia*: "An Imaginary Companion"; *Listenlight*: "Harvest Seam"; *Los Angeles Review*: "Resolution"; *Nthposition*: "Shallow Sky"; *Valparaiso Poetry Review*: "Fawns."

"Stone and Cloth and Paper," originally titled "Rainy Day Room," was commissioned for Henry Wadsworth Longfellow's 200th birthday by the Maine Historical Society. "Revelry" was commissioned as a mural for Sitwell's Café in Cincinnati, Ohio; published in the journals *88* and *Call: Review*; and reprinted as part of the essay entitled "Revising Revelry" in *American Poet* (Spring 2007) and in *The Poem, Revised*. "Architecture" (formerly "On Poetry and Architecture") was commissioned for the collaborative exhibition "Walking, Poems, Buildings," Poets House, New York, 2005. "A Wreath for Beltane," formerly "May Song," and "A Mabon Crown," formerly "A Crown of Leaves," commissioned for the Unitarian Universalist Society, appeared in the chapbook *Season Poems* (San Francisco: Calliope Press, 2001).

The Lost Poems "A Wreath of Time: For Anne Bradstreet," "An Imaginary

Song, premiered by Poets Theater of Maine, Portland, Maine, in a full-cast workshop production directed by Assunta Kent in 2011.

The translations of Anna Akhmatova's "The White Bird," "Cleopatra," and "Lot's Wife" appeared in *Cardinal Points*. The translations of Andrée Chedid's "Thirst" and "In Praise of Emptiness" appeared in *Poetry*. "A Fragment of Sappho" appeared in *Lofty Dogmas: Poets on Poetics* and in *A Poet's Craft: A Comprehensive Guide to Making and Sharing Your Poetry*.

ABOUT THE AUTHOR

Annie Finch is currently director of the Stonecoast MFA Program in Creative Writing at the University of Southern Maine. In 2009 she was the recipient of the Robert Fitzgerald Award. She has published six books of poetry, including one in translation, and several books on poetic technique.